Chronicles of a Coastal Town

Chronicles of a Coastal Town

Contributors

Gail Balentine
Darren Brown
Edward R. Brown
Sarah Corshia
John Cuffe
Meike Gourley

Stephen P. Hall
Lucy Keller
Michael Maler
Ed McFadden
Terri McFadden
Susan Milstein

Historic Beverly
2018

Copyright © 2018 by Historic Beverly

All rights reserved. This book or any portion thereof may not be reproduced or used in any manner whatsoever without the express written permission of the publisher except for the use of brief quotations in a book review or scholarly journal.

First Printing: 2018
ISBN 978-1-891906-19-0

Historic Beverly
117 Cabot St
Beverly, MA 01915

www.historicbeverly.net

Contents

Chapter 1: Here and There... 7
Chapter 2: Century by Century 26
Chapter 3: Getting Around..60
Chapter 4: Public Life 75
Chapter 4: Having Fun ....…82
Chapter 6: Making a Living ....…92
Chapter 7: Colorful Characters ....…124

Introduction

The idea for *Chronicles of a Coastal Town* came about when local historian Nancy Coffey suggested that gathering the articles published in the newsletters over the years might make an interesting book. The book covers a range of topics. The reader will learn about our maritime and agricultural roots, shoemaking and the coming of United Shoe Machinery Corp. Beverly's connection to the wider world are as broad as the last piracy attack in the Atlantic and the first atomic bomb. Some of the stories about people are sad, others funny and the people themselves are a cross-section from the humble to the powerful. We take a tour of the city to learn about the history of our neighborhoods and see pictures from the past. Our public life, religious institutions, transportation and how we have fun are touched on in both images and articles.

Although we look at events, individuals, and organizations from the earliest English settlement of 1636 into the 20th century, by the very nature of the original newsletter articles, this is not a comprehensive look at the history of Beverly. The authors whose work you will read, chose topics based on a myriad of reasons, including personal interest, exhibits that were on display, historic milestones and many others.

The articles were published in both the *Chronicle* and the e-newsletter from the early 2000s through the first half of 2018. The images used to illustrate the volume are part of the collection of Historic Beverly. It seems appropriate to publish this book in 2018, the 350th anniversary of Beverly's separation from Salem in 1668. Staff and volunteers worked very hard on this publication; we hope that you enjoy this glimpse into our community's rich history.

    Terri McFadden, Editor
    Sue Goganian, Director

Chapter 1: Here and There

Fish Flake Hill

Named after the flakes, or fish drying racks, that surrounded the waterfront, the name was given to the area when it was designated as a historic district in 1971. This is Beverly's earliest commercial area, first developed in the early 17th century when the ferry provided transportation to and from Salem. It is believed that Dixey's Tavern on Front Street was the place where a number of prominent citizens met in 1668 to choose the name 'Beverly' for their new town, just separated from Salem.

Preserving fish in the days before refrigeration required two steps, salting and then drying on 'flakes' - racks used to dry the fish. This fish flake stood on the harbor and was part of many fish drying yards in Beverly.

Clustered on this low hill are pre-Revolutionary War homes, a tavern and a chandlery - a business that sold provisions for ships, a factory that made candles and soap and Beverly's earliest commercial building – the warehouse that stands at the corner of Front and Water Streets. The area reached its height of development in the mid-18th century when merchants and sea captains built their quarter-acre wharves on Water Street. The first ship of George Washington's fleet was outfitted and sailed from Glover's Wharf and the harbor provided safe haven for privateers during the Revolutionary War. On Front Street, 13 residences are located, mostly built during the Georgian period between 1700-1780. One of the most impressive is the Captain Hugh Hill house, #50 Front, built in the 1780s by one of Beverly's most successful privateers.

A version of this article appeared in the November 2014 e-newsletter of the Beverly Historical Society.

Abbott Street and the Old Burial Ground

Take a walk down Abbott Street and you'll notice something odd – the cemetery is divided, lying on both sides of the street. Originally, the street was just a few blocks long, running from Lovett Street to Endicott Street. In 1869, a group lobbied for the extension of Abbott Street to Cabot Street, cutting through the burial ground. The project was voted down in five town meetings. Following the fifth, after opponents had left the hall, a motion to reconsider was made and passed. By the next morning, men were at work extending the street – moving gravestones, including those of Reverend John Hale and his family. By the early 20th century, Abbott Street had also been extended to Lothrop Street.

Originally the street was spelled 'Abbot' and was named in 1838 for Ariel Abbot, who served First Parish Church from 1803 to 1828. Abbot shepherded the church during the transition from Congregationalism to Unitarianism. Although radical differences of opinion arose regarding the new theology, it is a tribute to Reverend Abbot that a 'sizeable minority' who did not agree with him nevertheless followed his leadership and remained in the congregation.

Reverend John Hale Tombstone found in the walled section of the Abbott Street cemetery.

The Burial Ground, today known as the Abbott Street Cemetery, is the oldest cemetery in the city. People buried there include soldiers from the Colonial Era wars, a Minuteman who marched to Concord on April 19, 1775, two original members of the First Parish Church, and Elizabeth Brackenberry Patch, probably the first English female born in Massachusetts.

A version of this article appeared in May 2015 e-newsletter of the Beverly Historical Society.

Oddfellows Hall

The cornerstone for the Oddfellows Hall, the four-story High Victorian Gothic brick building located at 188-194 Cabot Street, was laid on Tuesday, September 8, 1874. A copper box 10x6x6 inches was set into the cornerstone. Little more than a year later the building was completed and dedicated, to great fanfare and a parade. The architect, J. Foster Ober, was the same man who designed the Briscoe Building at 3 Essex Street, and the contractors were the William Brothers of Beverly.

The bottom floor was designed to provide space for four businesses on the Cabot Street side, one on the Broadway side and one on the Wallis Street side – each of which are distinguished by an arch over large windows. The second floor was to provide office space, the third was the location for the headquarters of the Bass River Lodge, No. 141, Independent Order of Oddfellows, and on the fourth there was a banquet room/meeting hall.

While the architectural elements of the building on the outside and the original wood paneling and long staircases on the inside have been preserved, there has been extensive remodeling over the years to accommodate the many uses of the building. Over the years occupants have included: Ed Putnam's Boots and Rubbers, Ropes Drug Company, Klink's Bakery, and The Republican Club. In the 19th century Beverly citizens could visit the public gymnasium or the Western Union office. Rooms on the upper floor were used in 1909 for President Taft's summer offices. Public offices that have been located there include City Hall offices, social service agencies, and, from 1887 to 1912, on the Broadway side, the United States Post Office.

As it has for all its long life, in 2018 the building provides space for many businesses. The importance of the building was recognized in 1978, when it was added to the Register of Historic Places. Oddfellows Hall remains a mainstay on Cabot Street, providing a comfortable home for a myriad of local businesses and organizations.

A version of this article appeared in December 2017 e-newsletter of Historic Beverly.

Rantoul Street

In October 1851 Beverly selectmen proposed that a new street be cut downtown. It was to be about a mile long, running more or less parallel with Cabot Street, but straighter. The new street started near the "ancient ferry way" (Memorial Bridge) and ended at Cabot Street near Colon, where the Hay Market stood. It was hoped the broad thoroughfare would attract new businesses and homes.

Rantoul Street in the 19th century

By November 1852 the new street "was graded and ready for use", wrote Squire Robert Rantoul. He was gratified that the selectmen had decided to name it in his honor for the more than 50 years of service he had given the town in many capacities. Over the following years carriage factories, shoe factories, shops, schools, the post office, majestic Victorian

Rantoul Street in 1940

homes and triple decker houses for workers were gradually built, confirming Robert Rantoul's hope that the street would be an important center for Beverly. He would be pleased that, over its long history, Rantoul Street has remained so.

A version of this article appeared in January 2015 e-newsletter of the Beverly Historical Society.

The Public Life of Essex Street
By Terri McFadden

Essex Street begins in downtown Beverly and runs all the way to the Wenham line, it was first laid out in 1696, "two rods" or 33 feet wide. It leads off the tiny lane of Church Street, next to the First Parish Church and passes between the Beverly Common and the library to Dane Street. This short stretch has been important to the public life of the town from the earliest days.

Beverly's first schoolhouse was built on the Beverly Common in 1716. Prior to that time classes were held in the church or in rented space in private homes. The schoolhouse was moved to 50 Essex Street in 1754, where it still stands. As the population grew in the late 19th century and more schools were needed to educate the young, a series of buildings were constructed on this section of Essex Street. Several of these buildings have been torn down and those still standing are used for purposes other than public education. In 1873 the Briscoe building was built at 3 Essex Street to educate students from the downtown area. In 1899, it became Beverly's high school and for a time the public library was housed in this building. From the 1920s until the late 1960s the Briscoe building was Beverly's Junior High school. For several years it was also the headquarters of the North Shore Community College. A serious fire in the late 20th century gutted the building, but the exterior was saved and the interior rebuilt for use as a nursing home.

Standing on the common, Hardie Elementary school opened in 1899, the third public school on the site. It was named for Beverly's first schoolmaster, Samuel Hardie. Today the building is used by the Monserrat College of Art.

Boys at a drinking fountain on Beverly Common on the corner of Essex and Dane Streets.

The Beverly Common was originally used as the militia's training ground. From the earliest days of the colony every male from 18 to 45, except ministers and magistrates, was required to serve in the militia. At first the units were required to train every Saturday, with men who weren't proficient with their weapons to drill more often. This area, called the Training Ground well into the 19th century, was the site of such drills. The first powder house also stood here, until the second was built on Prospect Hill in 1801.

Across the street is the beautiful public library, designed by Cass Gilbert. Gilbert was a well-known architect whose commissions included the Minnesota state capitol and the U.S. Supreme Court. Beverly's library was constructed in 1913, a stately building of brick and marble. Over the Essex Street entrance is an unusual terra cotta ornamental half dome. The entire cost of the building was $100,000, which was raised locally by taxes and donations – a point of pride for the community at a time when wealthy financiers were paying for libraries across the country.

A version of this article appeared in the March 2015 e-newsletter of the Beverly Historical Society.

Robert Briscoe Leaves His Mark

By Stephen P. Hall

What's in a name? Many of us pass our time on earth with little remaining from our time on the planet. This is not true, of course of such national luminaries as Washington, Lincoln, and Jefferson.

Locally, similar acknowledgement was made by naming streets and buildings to stand witness to the mark of some individuals (Roger Conant, John Hale and Robert Rantoul for example) have made on our community.

But what does the average citizen of today really know of such people, most of whom survive only as names on street signs or public buildings? There has to be a reason why it was thought necessary and proper to honor these citizens of the past. One such honored individual was Robert Briscoe. His name has graced three buildings and four different schools over the years, and a street in the heart of downtown bears his name as well.

Robert Briscoe arrived in Beverly from the west of England in the late 1600s, first appearing in the town records in 1686. By 1691 he had married a local girl named Abigail Stone. During the next few decades he made his mark on the town with his public service. His elegant home stood nearly opposite the First Parish meeting house, on what now is part of Ellis Square. It was removed about 1798.

Robert Briscoe built a warehouse which still stands at the corner of Water and Front Streets-- one of Beverly's oldest commercial buildings. His success in business made it possible for him to donate funds for a variety of purposes and he gave of his time as well. Edwin Stone in his *History of Beverly* noted that Briscoe presented the town with a bell for the meetinghouse and a silver cup to the church. "He appears to have been a…public-spirited man, and his purse was always at the command of the town in anticipation of any want…He served as selectman, assessor, treasurer and representative, besides other important trusts in town and parish." When he died in 1729 he willed money to the minister of First Parish and more to help the poor of the town.

The first school named in his honor was in 1842 and called Briscoe Hall. It stood on Essex Street, not far from the site of his home. When the high school was built in 1875 on the same spot, it was called Briscoe School. It was converted in 1923 and named Briscoe Junior High School. In 1965 the Briscoe name was given to the middle school on Colon Street, when the Beverly High School moved to its current address at 100 Sohier Road. Next time you see a name on a building or a street sign, ask yourself who was that person? Why was he or she so honored? (Sohier anyone?) A bit of detective work might just answer the question.

A version of this article appeared in the Winter 2008 issue of the *Chronicle*.

Downtown Architecture

By Terri McFadden

Beverly City Hall, showing the Mansard roof, added in the late 19th century and removed in the 1930s.

The Mansard roof, sometimes called the curb roof, first became popular in 17th century France when Francois Mansert used it extensively in the public and private buildings that he designed. It was revived in France during the reign of Napoleon III as part of the Second Empire style of architecture, which also came into wide-spread use in America in the 1850s. Often used on large and grand buildings it was also popular for homes. A remodeling boom in America changed the original rooflines of many buildings, including Beverly City Hall, seen here with a fourth floor featuring the Mansard roof. City Hall was originally built in the 1780s using the Federalist style. It was then the three-story home of merchant Andrew Cabot. The added fourth floor, as well as the large addition off the back of the building drastically changed the building's character, though it added a large meeting room with a stage for public events. The fourth floor was removed in the early 20th century.

Not an easy style to define, the Queen Anne style house (left, 33 Washington) is sometimes described as "the one that you know when you see it." It became popular in the 1880s when the Industrial Revolution was transforming the country and well-to-do Americans were able to show off their success with these grand homes. Typical features include an asymmetrical façade, polygon towers, gables, wraparound porches, monumental chimneys and oriel and bay windows.

Many beautiful examples of this style can be found on Washington Street and Broadway and there are other homes in Beverly that illustrate the popularity of houses that reflect the wealth of the 19th and early 20th centuries.

Greek revival architecture was popular in American public buildings and private homes from the 1820s to the 1880s. This example of the architectural style at 19 Washington Street was built in 1838 for silversmith Oliver Trask (brother of Israel Trask, the Beverly silversmith known for Britannia ware). The house shows many features typical of the Greek revival style, including a temple-like façade with fluted Doric columns and the front-facing gable, which forms a pediment.

Versions of these articles were published in the August 2014, June 2015 and January 2017 e-newsletters of the Beverly Historical Society.

Essex Street: A trip to Centerville
By Terri McFadden

In the early 19th century the outskirts of town were just beyond the militia "training ground", what today we call Beverly Common. One of the oldest houses still standing is 111 Essex, built by fisherman and mariner William Woodbury about 1675. The property nearby became Beverly's poor farm in the late 19th century. Later, Hurd football stadium and a low-income housing complex were constructed here. Other old houses along the street include the William Cleaves house also built about 1675 at 252 Essex. William Cleaves (1654-1714) was married to Martha Corey. Tragically both Martha's father and stepmother were executed during the witchcraft crises of 1692. Her stepmother was hanged and her father, Giles Corey, was pressed to death – the court literally trying to force him to make a plea.

Today, one of the busiest spots along Essex is the Sterling Center of the YMCA. First opened in the late 20th century, the popularity of the Y has ensured that numerous additions have been made to the building. Daily, hundreds of children and adults visit the center to learn to swim, take fitness classes and enjoy its many programs.

Across the street, number 271, was built by planter William Livermore in 1671. His grandson and great-grandson, both named Livermore Whittredge, lived here and both men were active in the Revolutionary War. This property was a farm for many years and generations of "market gardeners" who lived here sold their produce in Boston.

The 1852 Walling map of Beverly shows that scattered along the length of the street were shoemaking shops – little "ten-footers" where one or two men would produce shoes. Most of the shops disappeared with the development of the downtown shoe factories. Just one ten-footer survives on this street, standing at 272 Essex.

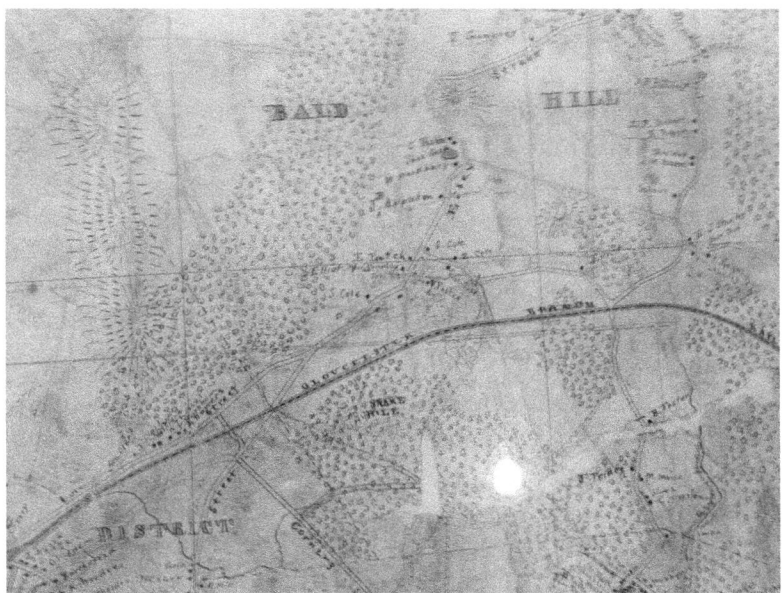

Centerville, once called Bald Hill, was until well into the 20th century, a series of farms which supplied produce to Boston and other regional cities. Oral histories tell of horse-drawn wagons leaving the farms at 3 or 4 in the morning and returning late in the afternoon. One woman said that during harvest her father would make the trip almost daily.

One of the oldest surviving schoolhouses in the city is 437 Essex – now the Bass River Community Center. The school opened its doors in 1870 and generations of children from the area received their education in this building. A branch of the public library was housed here as well. Nearby is the Centerville Hose House, built in 1903.

Further along the street is Long Hill, the summer home of Ellery Sedgwick, editor and publisher of the *Atlantic Monthly*. This Federal style house was begun in 1921 and incorporates beautiful wood trim removed from an early 19th century house in Charleston, South

Carolina. The gardens at Long Hill were designed by Sedgwick's wife, talented landscape designer Mabel Cabot Sedgwick. Renowned for their beauty, Mrs. Sedgwick designed the gardens as a series of "rooms," graced with statues and a variety of plants. The beauty of nature and the value of growing things is still an important activity on the former estate. Today it is the headquarters for the Trustees of the Reservations who are committed to preserving some of the wild places of our region. The property is farmed by The Food Project an organization that teaches youth the value of sustainable agriculture and the importance of affordable, high-quality food.

In a sense, the changing character of Essex Street though time mirrors the changes in the city as a whole. The value of education to the town shows in the numerous schoolhouses built along its length. Fishermen, farmers and shoemakers appear and then fade away as ways of making a living changed. In the 20th century farms were subdivided, and new homes built as Beverly's population increased. But through all the years and all the changes, the importance of community remains the same.

A version of this article appeared in the December 2015 e-newsletter of the Beverly Historical Society.

Cove Neighborhood: Ober Street
By Terri McFadden

Ober Street, in the Cove Neighborhood, is the route to Lynch Park, Beverly's popular seaside area. It is named for a family who first settled here in the 17th century. The name Ober probably derives from the French *Aubert*; members of this Protestant family fled from France to England in the 1500s to escape religious persecution. The first man appearing in Beverly with this name was Richard (1641-1716) who married Abigail Woodberry in 1671. Richard Ober was a 'shoresman' meaning he made his living from the fishing or shipping industries but did not himself go to sea. Among the beautiful old homes on the street are 11 Ober Street, the Captain Joseph Knowlton House, built about 1791; 48 Ober Street, the Hugh Woodberry House, dated to 1734; and number 52, the William Woodberry House, built about 1723.

Following her husband's death, Marie Evans commissioned an elaborate Italian garden to occupy the space where the guest house once stood. Image shows the garden on July 5, 1913.

The most prominent location on the street is Lynch Park, first settled in the early 17th century by the Woodberry family. In the 19th and 20th centuries this beautiful spot was divided into three estates, providing homes for wealthy families looking for cool summer breezes. Robert and Maria Evans eventually purchased all three houses, uniting them into one property. Their famous summer visitors included President William H. Taft and family – until Mrs. Evans grew tired of the commotion and had her guest house removed by barge to Marblehead. Mrs. Evans made good use of the land where the guest house once stood; she had the lovely Italian Garden installed there in the early 20th century. None of the homes that once stood on the property remain and the carriage house and former laundry are all that have survived of the estate buildings.

The city of Beverly purchased the property using funds from the David Lynch bequest and residents and visitors have enjoyed the Ober Street park since the 1940s.

A version of this article appeared in the September 2014 e-newsletter of the Beverly Historical Society.

Ryal Side

By Terri McFadden

Named after "cooper and cleaver of timber" William Ryall, who arrived in Salem in 1629, Ryall (or Royal) very soon left for Casco,

Maine, leaving only his name behind. This area was a part of Salem until 1753, the last section of land annexed to Beverly. Although today two well-traveled roads, Elliott Street and Bridge Street, pass through Ryal Side, for much of its history it was sparsely populated and isolated. It is nearly surrounded by water and until well into the 19th century travel was mainly achieved by boat.

Ryal Side in the 19th century, looking toward Elliott Street. Friend's Mill can be seen in the distance.

Alvah Bradstreet (born 1862), whose family farm lay alongside the river that straddled the Beverly/Danvers line, remembered that Ryal Side had "practically marked time for two hundred years" due to this isolation. There were land grants made here beginning in the 1630s, but it wasn't until the 19th century that Ryal Side really began to be developed. Prior to that there were several farms and the tidal mill, which operated for nearly 300 years across from today's Cummings Center, but not much else.

One of the more well-known people of Ryal Side was Ruben Kennison, who married into one of Beverly's old families, the Batchelders, who were among the earliest settlers. Kennison, originally from New Hampshire, married Apphia, daughter of Joshua Batchelder. Kennison was a member of the militia and he responded to the alarm at Lexington on the 19th of April 1775. Kennison was the only Beverly man who died that day, shot by the redcoats at Menotony, now Arlington.

In the 20th century, after the United Shoe Machinery Corporation arrived in town, the development of Ryal Side was ensured. Homes in the Shingleville neighborhood along McKay Street were built for executives. Slowly, over the course of decades new streets were laid out, filled with triple-deckers, Cape Cod houses and ranch-style homes for the workers of the huge factory.

The development of the Cummings Center at the site of the old USMC factory has kept Ryal Side moving forward with new businesses, shops and the construction of a large apartment building on the corner of McKay and Elliott, nearly on the site of the old miller's house – past and present merged.

A version of this article appeared in the August 2015 e-newsletter of the Beverly Historical Society.

North Beverly

From the earliest days of settlement into the 20th century North Beverly was an area of farms and small businesses. Dodge Street was named for an early 17th century family headed by Farmer William Dodge (c 1604-1685), known for his way with animals like cattle and horses. The way north was long called Dodge's Row and,

Dodge Street in an aerial view taken in the 1960s.

in the early 19th century, it was formally named Dodge Street. It wasn't until the 1960s, after the arrival of Route 128, that North Beverly began to be developed into the busy shopping area that we see today.

During the American Revolution one of Beverly's three companies of militia called the region home and quickly responded to the call of Lexington and Concord in April of 1775. During President George Washington's visit to New England the nation's hero stopped at the

Beverly Cotton Mill, now the site of the North Beverly Fire Station, to view the fabric that was being produced there.

In the 19th century Israel Porter Brown owned a farm on the land that today is North Shore Plaza. For many years Brown's field was the site of an annual Fourth of July bonfire, an event greatly enjoyed by generations of North Beverly residents. In the 1960s the property was seriously considered as the site for North Shore Shopping Center – now the mall in Peabody. Only the marshy nature of the ground kept the shopping center from being built here.

If you take time to observe, even in all the bustle of business and homes, vestiges of the early days can be seen. Several colonial era houses have survived – among them 580 Cabot Street, the beautiful Conant-Chipman house. This house was first the home of Exercise Conant, son of Beverly founder, Roger Conant. Later it became the home of the first minister to Second Congregational Church, the Reverend John Chipman, his wife Rebecca and their very large family. Tucked away next to the Second Congregational is the original cemetery. Here are buried some who were caught up in the late 17th century witchcraft crises, Revolutionary War soldiers, homemakers, ministers and doctors. It is their stories and the stories of their descendants that illuminate the life of North Beverly over the centuries.

A version of this article appeared in the May 2016 e-newsletter of the Beverly Historical Society.

Haskell Street and the Family that Inspired the Name
By Edward R. Brown

Haskell Street runs from Hale Street just west of St. Margaret's Church to Hart Street. It passes Dix Park and the Beverly Farms Cemetery. When the East Farms and West Farms school districts were combined in 1873, a new Beverly Farms School was built at the corner of Haskell Street and Webster Avenue. That wooden building was replaced by a brick school on the opposite corner, a building that was converted to 14 condominiums when the Farms School was closed. According to early 20th century historian Sidney Perley, the name Haskell Street dates back to 1841.

The Haskell family in Beverly can be found in the early years when it was still the Bass River Side section of Salem. Three

William Haskell House before it was restored.

brothers, Willian Sr., Roger and Mark, came to Salem from Bristol, England in the 1630s. William moved to Gloucester about 1645 and spent the rest of his life there. But Roger, a farmer, and his wife Elizabeth was granted land at Bass River and was head of one of the families listed as founders of Beverly. Roger Sr. died in 1667, the year before Beverly became a town; Elizabeth was one of the signers of the document that established the First Parish Church in 1667.

The old house at 680 Hale Street, not far from Haskell Street, known today as the William Haskell House, is believed to have been built in the early 18th century. It came into the Haskell family when William Haskell, son of Roger, married Ruth West, daughter of Captain Thomas West. Ruth's father conveyed the property as part of her dowry on March 1, 1689/90. The land had originally been included in the 300-acre farm of Thomas's father, John, one of the first selectmen of Beverly, who had acquired the 300 acres from John Blackleach. Of John West's three sons, only Thomas was alive when John died in 1683, so the farm went to him. When William Haskell died, the house was left to his 16-year old son, William Jr. An old newspaper account has it that six generations of Haskells lived there. According to Perley, Thomas West had a sawmill on Chubb's Creek at the northwesterly side of Haskell Street about 1690. What is now Hart Street from Hale to the Wenham line was originally a private cart road for the Wests.

For Beverly, as in most nearby communities, where one sat during sabbath services was determined largely by social status. Men and women did not sit together, and children often were forced to squat uncomfortably on the pulpit steps under the stern gaze of an elder. In one 18th century "seating" of the meeting house, the committee determined that Robert Haskell was to share the prestigious first pew with Colonel Robert Hale, Joshua Herrick, Robert Morgan, James Woodberry, Benjamin Cleaves and Henry Herrick. It is interesting to note that except for Cleaves, a street in Beverly bears the name of each of those families.

A version of this article was published in the Winter 2014 issue of the *Chronicle*

Goodbye Long Pond
by Edward R. Brown

On February 16, 1635/6 the town of Salem granted 300 acres at what is now Beverly Farms to John Blackleach, who later transferred his grant to John West. The latter moved there and established a farm. Then in 1666/7, Salem gave to West perpetual rights to a pond on the property and to what soon was named West's Beach. With establishment of the Town of Beverly in 1668, the old Salem grants stood.

The pond, called Long Pond or Blackleach's Pond, came so close to the ocean that there was barely room to site the highway to Manchester. A map published by Sidney Perley shows how close the road was to the beach. In 1696 a storm broke through the fragile barrier, causing the pond to drain into the sea, never to refill. That event also washed out the road, making it nearly impossible to travel between Beverly and Manchester and beyond. Citizens at the town meeting in Manchester on October 19th, 1696 complained that the road "on the beach namely West's Beach being broken up by reason of the pond breaking into the sea...makes that part of the way very hazardable and difficult for travelers."

Rectifying the situation took a cooperative effort between Beverly and Manchester. Beverly appointed a committee of Andrew Elliott, Paul Thorndike, William Raymond and Samuel Corning to join with Manchester representatives, John Siblee, Robert Leach, Samuel Allen Sr. and John Ley. Meeting on March 19, 1697 they agreed on a new highway across the land of Thomas West, heir of John West, and a piece of common land. That road probably closely coincides with the present West Street.

A version of this article appeared in the July 2014 e-newsletter of the Beverly Historical Society.

Chapter 2: Century by Century

Old Planters

Detail of the painting, Beverly in 1700, *painted by Avis Thomas in 2016. It depicts the town as it may have appeared in the colonial period when the primary occupations were farming and fishing.*

Beverly began in 1635 when a grant of 1000 acres was given to five men, Roger Conant, John Balch, John Woodberry, William Trask, and Peter Palfrey – the "Old Planters." They were part of a group of men and women who had first settled in Gloucester in 1623. The fishing station begun there soon failed and Conant persuaded five families to stay in the New World and try making a living as farmers. They settled in Naumkeag, today's Salem, for a decade before crossing the Bass River and starting a new community. The Balch House was built in 1680 on the site of John Balch's original 1636 house. A garrison house was reportedly the first building built in Beverly by the colonists. It stood on Ober Street on today's Lynch Park until it was torn down in the early 19th century

Regulating the "Superfluous and Unnecessary"
By Terri McFadden

Many people today are wary of government intervention in their lives; some long for the old days when, as they believe, citizens had more freedom. For our seventeenth-century ancestors, such freedom was certainly not part of their lives. Rather, the Puritans who settled here in the 1600s hoped to regulate the sin out of the community in their efforts to establish a perfect society. John Winthrop famously described the community they hoped to establish "As a city upon a hill" – a place that the whole world would look at and marvel.

Sumptuary laws were passed at various times by the Massachusetts General Court regulating extravagance in food and dress – with clothing the main focus of regulation. These laws harken back to the medieval period when many countries attempted to enforce the status and behavior of their people.

In seventeenth-century New England there was real concern that people were wasting money on unnecessary, fancy clothing. In 1634 the legislature decreed that due to the expense of "new and immodest fashions" people should refrain from wearing lace or decorating their clothing with gold or silver threads. Slashed sleeves and "cutwork" were forbidden, as were beaver hats and double ruffs. "Greate sleeves" [of] more than half an ell" (22 inches wide) were also forbidden. It wasn't just the expense. Leaders attempted to restrain immodest behavior. Garments with short sleeves were not to be worn lest "the nakedness of the arme" be exposed. The court promised that such scandalous garments would be confiscated and any tailor who added lace or any forbidden item would be fined.

The issue was again brought before the legislature a few years later when the lawmakers acknowledged the trouble they were having restraining the excesses in apparel in both men and women. This time they chose to address those in "mean condition" – the poor. Lawmakers expressed the opinion that since those who were well-off had obviously been blessed by God, if they wanted to wear fancy clothing it wasn't the court's place to restrain them. However, the "blind and stubborn" poor people of the Commonwealth needed a firm hand to keep them from wasting their money on finery. Anyone with a net worth of less than 200 pounds was not allowed to wear any of the items on the forbidden list, which was expanded to include "great boots" for men and silk hoods and scarfs for women. Fines of ten shillings were imposed for infractions.

Abruptly, in 1644 the court issued the following statement: "It is ordered, that all those former orders made about apparel [sic] and lace are hereby repealed." With this statement, it appears that the lawmakers were conceding that there some things that can't be legislated. But into the 1660s other laws were enacted to try, at the very least, to keep children and servants in garb deemed correct "for their station." The desire to regulate society remains with us, though not in our clothing. It is an interesting exercise to contemplate the similarities to lawmakers who today wish to restrict choices with those laws enacted by our Puritan forebears.

A version of this article was printed in the Fall 2015 issue of the *Chronicle*.

Exercise and Sarah Conant – Travels in New England
By Terri McFadden

We have a tendency to think that people in colonial times did not move much from place to place. But in fact, they moved often, settling new territory, sometimes in dangerous frontier communities. In the case of Exercise and Sarah Conant, it appears they moved for reasons common today; a less strenuous way of making a living and living near family.

The Conant-Chipman House

Puritans often chose unusual names for their children. Old Planter, Roger Conant and his wife Sarah picked the name "Exercise" for their youngest son, born in Bass River Side (Beverly) in 1637. His life followed a typical pattern for a person of his time and station. He was granted freeman status in 1663, enabling him to vote and to serve on juries. He was married by 1667 to Sarah and they had their first child the following year. The couple settled in Beverly where they built a house which still stands at 634 Cabot Street. He was a yeoman farmer and for the next 28 years they farmed and raised their six children, all of whom were baptized at First Parish Church.

Land owning males in colonial times were expected to participate in local and colony activities and Exercise Conant was no exception. Some of his public duties included serving as a representative from Beverly to the General Court. He was appointed a member of the committee charged with "…prevent[ing] tippling and drunkenness" among the town's citizens, supervising ten families. During the Canadian expedition of 1690, Conant gained the rank of lieutenant, and he was known by that title for the rest of his life. He also oversaw estate inventories for the Quarterly Court of Essex County. Altogether it seems Exercise Conant was an upstanding and useful citizen.

With their children grown and married, Exercise and Sarah moved to Windham, Connecticut, where their son Josiah had settled. They purchased a house and 1000 acres, but stayed just one year, moving on to Lebanon, Connecticut where they lived for five years. In 1701 they moved yet again, this time to Boston. Exercise was now in his 60s and perhaps was hoping to find a less arduous way of making a living. He obtained a license to sell "all sorts of drink" – ironic considering his previous task of "preventing tippling." Exercise joined the Boston watch, becoming one of its paid overseers. He was also paid to regulate burials and ensuring that bells were rung to indicate the hour. After 11 years away from their home town, Exercise and Sarah finally requested that their membership be moved from Beverly to Boston's North Church.

One more move lay ahead. After 17 years in Boston, they moved back to Windham to live with son Josiah. Sarah's health may have been precarious; she died very soon afterward. Exercise lived to the great age of 85 dying in 1722. His gravestone can still be seen in the churchyard in Mansfield, Connecticut.

A version of this article appeared in the Spring 2015 issue of the *Chronicle*.

When John Hale Came to Beverly
By Edward R. Brown

When Beverly was still a part of Salem known as Bass River Side, attendance at church services in Salem, which were mandatory for all residents, whether members of the Salem Church or not, was both difficult and often dangerous. It involved either paddling one's own canoe or waiting with the family for the flat-bottomed ferry, which was open to the weather and could carry only a limited number of horses.

So about 1656 the Salem Church allowed the Bass River residents to build a small meetinghouse on their side and employ a "teaching officer" to conduct Sabbath services. They still had to go to Salem for such ordinances as baptisms and Communion services. Bass River first employed in succession two brothers named Hobart, and built a parsonage for the second, Jeremiah, who seems to have left under less than friendly circumstances.

So in 1664 the village hired 28-year-old John Hale, a native of Charlestown and a graduate of Harvard College, which qualified him for the ministry. That same year he married Rebecca Byley of Salisbury and they would have two children, Rebecca (Becky) born in 1666 – she died in 1681 -- and Robert two years later. Although he was not as yet ordained, the people of Bass River agreed to pay him a salary of 70 English pounds per year and supply his firewood, an arrangement similar to that accorded a minister in nearby towns. John Hale and the people of Beverly hit it off well, and when Salem agreed in 1667 to allow an independent church on this side of the river, John Hale was ordained to be its pastor. With a church in hand, Mr. Hale and his friends succeeded in 1668 to petition the Great and General Court to make them a separate town, which the court named Beverly.

John Hale would remain in Beverly as its spiritual leader until his death in 1700, except for an absence in 1690 when the General Court tapped him as chaplain for the military expedition to Quebec, over the objections of the townspeople. After his first wife died in 1683, he married Sarah Noyes, youngest child of the first teacher of the church in Newbury, and she gave him four children. John Hale had acquired land of his own, and in 1694 a grateful town gave him ownership of the parsonage. Needing space for his growing family, in that same year he built a house. It is a matter of conjecture whether this was entirely new construction or an addition to the existing ministry house, although what evidence there is points toward the former. There have been two additions to the present Hale House.

John Hale seems to have been popular with the exception of an incident in 1678 when his live-in maid, Margaret Lord, robbed the ministry house while terrorizing his children, taking her spoil to her friend Dorcas Hoar, whose side occupations as both a fortune teller and receiver of stolen goods got her into dangerous trouble when the witchcraft delusion of 1692 broke out. While he succeeded in keeping Beverly largely out of the spotlight, John Hale was nevertheless caught up in the hysteria as a witness, and he along with others saved Dorcas Hoar on the day before her scheduled execution. When it was all over and people had regained their senses, it was John Hale who sat down in the present day Hale House to write the book that became his legacy. *A Modest Enquiry into the Nature of Witchcraft* was intended to prevent a repetition of the fatal mistakes made by the Salem witch court.

After John Hale was fatally stricken while inspecting family property in Charlestown following a destructive storm, Robert Hale, then 32, inherited the family homestead. Sarah Noyes Hale had died before her husband, so the four orphaned children from the second marriage were sent to live with Noyes relatives in Newbury, and they are ancestors of a family that has spread far and wide. What became known as Hale farm remained in the family well into the 20th century. Robert Hale Jr. (Col. Robert Hale) succeeded his father. On his death in 1767 he willed it to his only surviving child, Elizabeth Hale Ives, with the provision that on her death it would pass to his beloved grandson, Robert Hale Ives. When the latter died at sea, his widow and their four children lived there until the mother's death, after which an aunt from Salem swooped in to gather up the orphaned children and take them to her home.

Hale Farm, rear view about 1907

Over the next 70 years or so, Hale Farm, which now boasted 100 acres or more running to the ocean was rented in succession to three tenant farmers –Hale Hilton, Peter Hill and Alden Harris – until the early 1840s. By then ownership had passed to a grandson of one of those orphaned Ives children, Thomas Poynton Bancroft. Mr. Bancroft, a wealthy Boston cotton merchant, decided to fix up the old house and make the place into his summer estate. He and his son, Robert Hale Bancroft made the changes that turned John Hale's old home into the showplace it is today. With the death of Robert Hale Bancroft's widow in 1937, her daughter sold off much of the land for house lots (think Bancroft Avenue) while the old house and the surrounding lot were sold to the Beverly Historical Society for $5,000. That organization, now named Historic Beverly, retains the responsibility for preserving it as an historic landmark in Beverly.

A version of this article appeared in the Fall 2018 issue of the *Chronicle*.

The Retreat from Long Island – 1776
By Terri McFadden

In early August of 1776, Glover's Regiment, then stationed at Beverly, was ordered to march to New York. The largest portion of this militia regiment was filled by Marblehead men, but men from other area towns also served; more than 100 of them from Beverly. Moses Brown was the captain of one regimental company comprised largely of Beverly men. Brown kept a diary during his 18 months of fighting in New York and New Jersey, which despite its spare style, gives a great deal of information.

Initially the regiment was held in reserve, but when Washington made the decision to retreat to Manhattan, he called on two Essex County regiments, Glover's 14th and Israel Hutchinson's 27th to ferry the army to safety. Although these units were part of the army, the men serving were mainly experienced seamen and fishermen, able to execute the complicated amphibious operation.

Boats large enough to move the 9000-man army, their horses and equipment were obtained while skirmishes with the British continued and enemy siege lines were being dug nearby in preparation for the final onslaught against the American lines. Upriver the largest fleet assembled in the 18th century waited for a favorable breeze to attack Washington's forces. The British had high expectations that this battle would end the rebellion.

In darkness and near complete silence the Americans began moving men, horses and cannon to the banks of East River. Wheels and oars were muffled, orders were issued in whispers and the Essex County soldiers manned the boats. For nine hours under the cover of darkness they rowed the army across the river. Just a few men, officers and General Washington remained when daylight broke. A thick morning fog, called "providential" in reports of the day, arose and the last boatloads were transported to safety. Captain Brown wrote with typical understatement: "Retreated from L Island 14th Regt assisted all night." It is not an exaggeration to say that the incredible feat of the Essex

County regiments preserved the Continental Army and perhaps the fight for our independence.

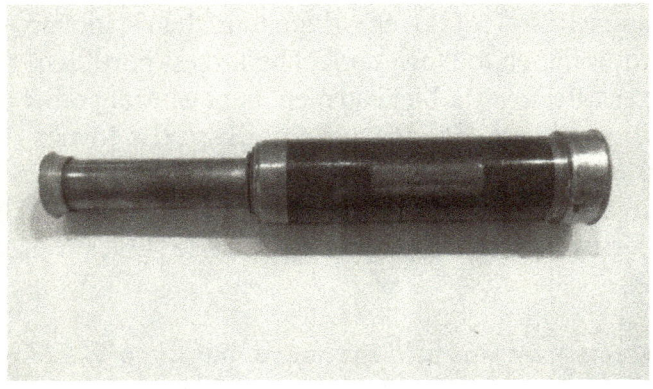

Captain Moses Brown used this telescope during the 1776 campaign with Glover's Regiment.

A version of this article appeared in the August 2014 e-newsletter of the Beverly Historical Society.

A Sad, but Common Tale

By Terri McFadden

Abagail (Stephens) Dike was an ordinary wife and mother, beloved by her family and an esteemed member of the Beverly community. We know a little about her life and death because her nephew, Stephens Baker, mentioned her in his memoir. She was born in 1757 and married John Dike in 1777. Over the course of 20 years she gave birth to 11 children, only five of whom survived childhood. In 1797 she gave birth to twins and both children and their mother died as a result of complications of childbirth. In preparation for her funeral she was dressed in white, which exactly matched her pale face according to her nephew, and she was placed in a plain coffin holding a newborn baby in each arm.

As a very old man Baker vividly remembered these details and more. He wrote that her funeral procession was unusually long, stretching from her home on Vestry Street to the burial ground – today called

Abbott Street Cemetery. In those days no carriages were used, instead people walked by twos behind the black-painted coffin, borne by four men. Called bearers, these men were hired to carry the coffin to the cemetery, mounted on a bier. They were paid, according to Baker, "fifty cents and furnished with intoxicating drinks...." The coffin was covered by a black velvet pall that had six tassels sewn to it. The tassels were held by six pallbearers, who were selected "because their age matched that of the deceased." For more than 80 years Stephens Baker remembered his beloved aunt, the sadness of her death in childbirth and the solemn nature of her funeral. A simple stone standing alone next to the railing in Abbott Street Cemetery was placed in memory of Abagail and John Dike and their six children who died so very young.

A version of this article appeared in the September 2015 e-newsletter of the Beverly Historical Society.

Set at Liberty
By Terri McFadden

"...have made diligent Enquiry into the Exact Number of the Negro Slaves both males and females sixteen years and upwards."

These are among the earliest words written about African-Americans in Beverly, the result of a census of "Negro Slaves" ordered by the Massachusetts General Court in 1754. The "diligent Enquiry" found that Beverly had 28 slaves – 12 males and 16 females over the age of 16. The total population of the town was about 2000. At this time slaves in Massachusetts made up nearly 2% of the total population. There was a deep-seated belief, harkening back to the Puritan belief in predestination, that blacks were in servitude because God willed it so. Robert Rantoul wrote that although many "conscientious persons" of the time would not engage in active trade with Africa, they would buy slaves if they were offered for sale, "...because they supposed that an education in a land of gospel light was preferable to one in heathenish darkness."

Slavery was never an important source of labor in Massachusetts. However, there were more slaves in the coastal towns than in the inland communities. In the 17th century, when farming was the most common occupation, there were fewer slaves. As maritime trade became more important in the early 1700s the slave population increased, peaking in Beverly just before the American Revolution at nearly 80 individuals.

A rather surprising number of references to one particular local black family can be found in personal memoirs, census and court records. This is the family of Juno Larcom and her husband Jethro Thistle. Juno was half native American and half black. Her Indian mother was stolen from North Carolina and sold in New England. Juno was born about 1724 and was purchased in Portsmouth, New Hampshire by Captain Henry Herrick of Beverly. When his daughter Mary, married John West in 1732, little Juno went with her mistress, although Herrick retained ownership of her. John West died in 1745 and in 1750 Mary West was married for the second time to David Larcom.

In his will Captain Herrick named Mary as Juno's owner. Since a woman's property legally belonged to her husband, Juno's owner was, in fact, David Larcom. It was at this time that she became known as Juno Larcom. For a short time, she used the surname Freeman, but she later returned to Larcom.

In 1751 Juno married Jethro Thistle, slave of Jeffery Thistle. Over the next twenty years the couple had 12 children, 11 of whom survived to adulthood. Juno and Jethro and all their children were baptized at Beverly's First Parish church where they "claimed the covenant" – becoming members of the congregation. The homes where the Larcoms and Thistles lived were near each other in the Pride's Crossing area of Beverly, and it is possible that the couple were able to live together for at least part of their marriage. During the course of Jethro's life, he was sold twice more, both to Beverly men. In 1777, while still a slave, Jethro joined the Continental Army, fighting for liberation from the rule of Great Britain. Jethro served for about a year in the campaigns in upstate New York. He died at Valley Forge in the brutal winter of 1778, at about 54 years old.

A story passed down in the white Larcom family suggested that when David Larcom realized that slavery would soon be abolished in the commonwealth he began selling his slaves. It is more likely that financial reverses caused him to take this step and he sold two of Juno and Jethro's children. One, a daughter was sold out-of-state, to a buyer in New York. The loss of these children seems to have spurred Juno to action.

At this time there were a number of lawsuits brought in Massachusetts by slaves seeking their freedom. Public sentiment in Massachusetts had turned against the idea of slavery and most of these suits were successful. In July 1774 Juno Larcom brought suit against David Larcom seeking freedom for herself and her children. She told the court that she had served her mistress for more than 46 years and that her master had sold several of her children and had beaten her. She finished by saying: *Judge Ye Weather or noe I hadent ort to be set at Liberty.*"

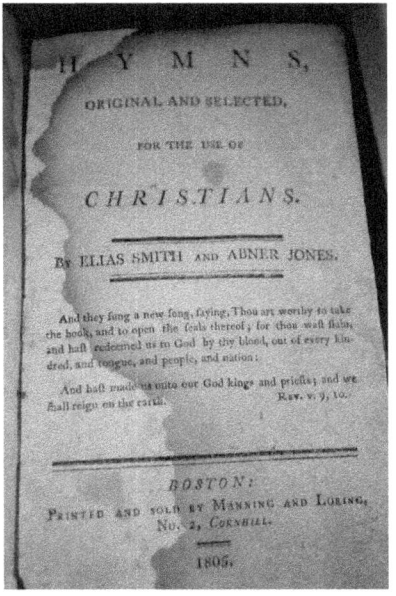

First page of Cloe Turner's Hymnal. Cloe was the youngest child of Juno Larcom and Jethro Thistle.

Before the case was decided by the court, David Larcom died and the lawsuit was dismissed. But perhaps the most unusual part of the matter happened next. According to probate records Juno and her family "claim'd their freedom." The white Larcom family accepted this and provided a home for Juno and her large household, near the road at Pride's Crossing. In 1790 in the first census of the United States Juno is listed as the head of household. Over the years the numbers of people in her home varied between eight and eleven. Their lives couldn't have been easy. Receipts and personal stories tell us that the Larcom family members took in laundry, worked as housekeepers and found jobs in the maritime trades, rarely making enough to make ends meet. Beverly selectman records show that the family received 'outside' assistance from the town of firewood and food – indicating that they were able to stay in their home.

37

Only one of Juno's children, Flora, who had returned from slavery in New York, was forced to live in the workhouse.

For well over 100 years this family lived and worked in Beverly. Juno lived until the great age of 92. Her last surviving child, Chloe, died at age 95. Writer Lucy Larcom knew them and wrote that though they were well-respected, the black Larcom family always seemed out of place. Whether this was true or not, the descendants of Juno Larcom and Jethro Thistle could look back with pride at the stand their ancestors took in their quest for liberty.

A version of this article appeared in the Summer 2012 issue of the *Chronicle*.

Celebrating the Peace – 1815
By Edward R. Brown

On Christmas Eve, 1814, the Treaty of Ghent put an end to the hated War of 1812, the last armed conflict between Britain and the United States, which had ruined Beverly's economy and caused much hardship and suffering to its citizens. But it wasn't until Monday February 13, 1815, that word reached Beverly, setting off a town-wide celebration.

Captain Robert Rantoul, commanding the Volunteer Artillery Association, called a special meeting at the Gun House for 2 p.m. The men obtained 18 carriages, dragged their guns to the top of Watch Hill, located above the Common, and made sure everyone in town could hear their salute to peace. That was only the beginning of a celebration that ran well into the night. William Endicott, a teenager at the time wrote: "Peace was declared in February 1815, and there was a great celebration. The two 18-pounders down on the shore fired all afternoon." Writing many years later, citizen-soldier Stephens Baker, a sergeant in the town's militia, said the celebration in Beverly exceeded the joy caused by the news of the end of the Civil War in 1865. The military company commanded by Captain William Thorndike escorted a parade of townspeople to the First Parish meeting house for a service of thanksgiving. Wrote Baker: "After the service at the church the Infantry escorted a large number of the citizens to partake of a public dinner in the Town Hall on Briscoe Street, which occupied the afternoon and evening in drinking toasts and making speeches. In the evening all the buildings of the principal street were illuminated, bonfires on the principal hills burned, the Band playing in the streets, and everybody seemed to be happy as it was indeed an occasion for joy."

For a year the economically shattered town of fewer than 5000 had lived in fear of attack from the sea. Some 26 Beverly soldiers and sailors lost their lives in combat ashore and at sea. As many as 84 Beverly sailors suffered the horror of captivity in British prisons, half of them in the notorious Dartmoor Prison. Two brothers, George and John Tittle, were captured and sold into slavery in Algiers, never to be heard from again. In 1815 Beverly indeed welcomed peace.

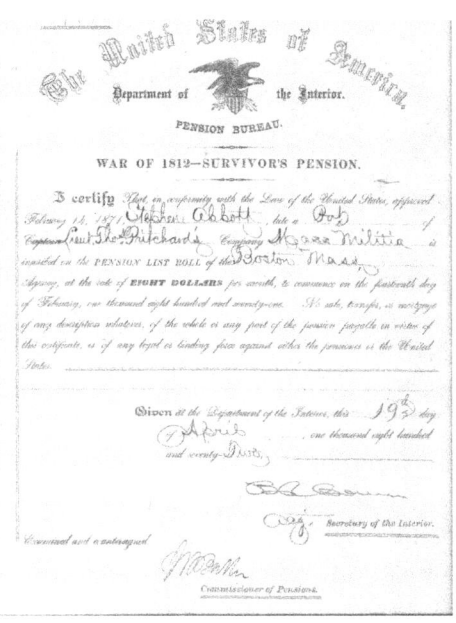

Awarded in 1872, this War of 1812 survivors pension was approved for Stephen Abbott, who served in the Massachusetts Militia.

A version of this article appeared in the March 2015 e-newsletter of the Beverly Historical Society.

The Year Without a Summer

By Edward R. Brown

They called it "the year with a summer." Old-timers later referred to it as "Eighteen Hundred and Froze to Death." More than two hundred years ago, in 1816, spring never came; summer was brief and mostly cold. Summer snow was reported and early frosts destroyed crops that farmers had planted. Widespread crop failures and famines ensued across eastern North America and throughout much of Europe. Some people feared it heralded the end of the world.

Blame for this global disaster was placed on the 1815 eruption of Mount Tambora, located on the island of Sumbawa in the Dutch East Indies (Indonesia). The massive volcanic eruption killed thousands in the region and sent tons of ash into the upper atmosphere. By the next year, the winds had blown the ash in a swath around the world, cooling the climate and causing wide-spread crop failure.

By June the *Salem Gazette* had taken note of the strange weather. On June 11th the paper told its readers; "Our cold weather and even frosts still continue. About 10 o'clock on Saturday we had a slight snow. On Sunday morning ice was drawn from the well at the toll-house on the Turnpike…and there was frost again on Sunday evening…in the upper part of this state, on Saturday, large icicles [were] pending and the foliage of the forest was blasted by the frost."

Though the local weather improved for a time, other regions were not so fortunate. Corn crops in western Massachusetts were so damaged they were not worth harvesting. Scarcity of grain caused prices to rise, and people went hungry. Food riots were reported in Europe. It was estimated that worldwide more than 90,000 people died as result of hunger or disease the year after the eruption.

That disastrous summer did produce one important cultural note. Mary Shelley and some of her literary friends were vacationing in Geneva, Switzerland that June. Due to the severity of the weather they were forced to remain indoors. To pass the time, they decided on a contest to see who could write the scariest story. Shelley's submission, *Frankenstein*, so impressed the others that she expanded on it and set it off to her publisher.

A version of this article appeared in the July 2016 e-newsletter of the Beverly Historical Society.

Stop Thief! - Horse Thievery in Beverly

By Edward R. Brown

Stealing horses in the 19th century did not only occur in the Wild West. It happened right here in Beverly. In the *Salem Gazette* on Tuesday, August 13, 1816, an advertisement headed "Stop Thief!" reported that on the previous Saturday night John P. Webber's mare was stolen from her stable in Beverly, along with a new saddle a double bridle. The missing horse was a dark bay mare, 14 hands high, with a white streak on her face, one white foot, "and a peculiar trick of throwing her head up and down."

The owner, John Webber (left), was a young family man, 32 years old. He and his wife, Desire Ellingwood, had at the time five children (they would have a total of 10). In addition to the loss of a valuable animal and its tack, it must have stung to have the horse stolen right out of the barn.

The thief reportedly was seen riding north in the "upper" parish, (North Beverly). The next morning, at Caldwell's Tavern in Newburyport, Mr. Weber offered a reward of $10 for the return of his mare and $20 for the apprehension of the miscreant. The ad was repeated in the following two issues of the *Gazette*, but subsequent papers do not reveal whether the aggrieved Beverly man recovered his horse.

A version of this article appeared in the April 2016 e-newsletter of the Beverly Historical Society.

"Dead Cats Don't Mew": Pirates Attack the Brig *Mexican*

By Terri L. McFadden

On August 29, 1832 the brig *Mexican* sailed out of Salem under the command of John G. Butman of Beverly. The vessel was bound for Brazil with a cargo of saltpeter, tea and ten cases filled with coin worth $20,000 – an enormous amount of money, equivalent to approximately $475,000 today. In those days it wasn't uncommon to carry coin – some foreign merchants would only accept money, not goods in trade.

Three weeks passed uneventfully, but on the 20th of September a schooner was sighted. Hours passed with the two ships sailing near each other. Captain Butman became concerned with the "strange sail." His worry proved justified when the schooner fired "a gun to leeward…." The American ship, with its crew of 12, was no match for the pirate vessel, with as many as 60 men aboard and several guns.

The *Panda* was a former privateer from Colombia. Pedro Gilbert, who had moved from privateering to piracy, commanded the vessel. His act of piracy was one of the last recorded in the Atlantic. Gilbert ordered Captain Butman and four of his men moved to the *Panda* for questioning. When asked what was in the hold, Butman answered, "saltpetre and tea." Evidently the pirates didn't believe this. After returning to his vessel Butman was threatened by

From a booklet c. 1834 relating the trial of the pirates from the Panda. *It shows the mate from the American ship begging for his life.*

two pirates armed with knives who demanded "Money, Money." Captain Butman was forced to reveal the location of the coin and his men were beaten to make them remove the cases faster. One crewman, who understood Spanish, heard Captain Gilbert questioned as to what the pirates should do with the prisoners. Gilbert answered: "Dead cats don't mew. You know what to do." The Americans were locked in the hold while the pirates shredded the sails, set the *Mexican* on fire and sailed off with their treasure. The Americans survived only because one small skylight had been overlooked, allowing the crew to escape before the ship went down.

Several years later, twelve of the pirates were captured and brought to Boston for trial. Benjamin Larcom (brother of local writer, Lucy Larcom) was among the crew; he testified at the trial, identifying "Ruiz the piratical carpenter." Understandably the voyage of the *Mexican* was Benjamin's first and last sea voyage. Following the terrifying events of 1832, he happily stayed ashore. Captain Pedro Gilbert and three of the 12 men tried with him were found guilty and hanged for their crimes in 1835.

A version of this article appeared in the October 2015 *Chronicle* of the Beverly Historical Society.

Preserving the Union

By Darren Brown

The years of the American Civil War were the most turbulent times in the history of the United States. During the election of 1860, Abraham Lincoln campaigned against the expansion of slavery beyond the states where it already existed. Following Lincoln's election as president, seven Southern states seceded from the Union and created the Confederate States of America. Four more states followed after Lincoln's call for troops after the attack on Fort Sumter, in Charleston, South Carolina. Farming villages, seaport towns and industrial cities sent more than 2,200,000 men in support of the Union. An estimated 620,000 died and millions of lives were forever altered.

Beverly, like other northern towns, provided troops to fight for the Union cause. Between 1861 and 1865, 735 men from Beverly joined the army or navy. More than ten percent of the population of the town served, ninety men over the quota. Seventy-four of them died and many more fell ill or were wounded, some succumbing after their return home. There were 32 men commissioned as officers during the conflict, most of them promoted from the ranks. A Beverly man, Lieutenant Moses Herrick had the unhappy distinction of being the first amputee of the war.

Captain Francis Porter was instrumental in having Beverly men become the first in the state to answer President Lincoln's call to arms. In 1861 he was a captain in Beverly's Light Infantry unit. On April 16th he received a telegram from Boston ordering him to muster his men and have them report to Boston the next day. Captain Porter contacted his men, visiting some of them personally, to tell them to prepare to leave early the next morning. After roll was called the next day, he and his men, with many townspeople cheering them on, marched to the Beverly Depot, where they boarded the 8:40 train. The Beverly troop became Company E of the newly organized Eighth Massachusetts Infantry Regiment. They were ordered to North Carolina where they were assigned mostly defensive duty and fought with rebel troops at Blount's Creek. In July of 1863, after a forced march to Gettysburg, Pennsylvania, they arrived after General Lee had returned south, thus missing the battle. Francis Porter was promoted and finished the war as a colonel.

As the country began the long road to healing, memorial societies and charities sprang up, encouraging people to preserve the narratives and mementos to "illustrate the heroism and self-sacrifice…" of those who had fought. Citizens donated money to assist with what the *Beverly Citizen* called "the after-clap of war", including funds to help the freed slaves, orphaned children both in the north and the south, and to build hospitals and soldier's homes to assist the wounded.

The veterans from Beverly who returned home at the war's conclusion attempted to pick up where they had left off. Those who were physically able returned to their jobs as shoemakers, machinists, sailors or farmers, though their lives had been forever changed by what they had witnessed. Many would maintain lifelong friendships with comrades with whom they had fought to preserve the United States and eradicate slavery. The Grand Army of the Republic (GAR) became the nation's largest Union veteran's organization. GAR Post #89 in Beverly was founded in June 1869 and named after John H. Chipman, Jr., one of the brave soldiers from Beverly who already "crossed the river" following the war due to a disease he had contracted while in Libby prison. The GAR played a prominent role locally as well as nationally, establishing pension legislation, and promoting charitable causes for veterans, widows and orphans. The GAR also raised money to erect monuments in nearly every town and city in order to keep the memory of the cause alive. Decoration Day (now Memorial Day) was begun by the GAR. Here in Beverly the community first gathered to decorate the graves of veterans on June 6, 1868. In all these ways the memory of the sacrifice made by the men who fought and their families at home was remembered. A century and half later, it is no less important.

Soldier John Hale Chipman, Jr. was captured at Weldon Railroad, Virginia in August, 1864. Lieutenant Chipman was held captive at the infamous Libby Prison in Richmond, where he contracted typhoid fever. At the end of the war Chipman mustered out as a captain and returned to Beverly. He never recovered his health and died in 1866. The Grand Army of the Republic Post #89 was named in his honor.

Versions of this article appeared in the *Chronicle* Fall 2008 and the March 2015 e-newsletter of the Beverly Historical Society.

Beverly Soldier Fell at Gettysburg

By Edward R. Brown

The Central Cemetery gravestone of Sergeant Charles Francis Ferguson was repaired and rededicated in 2014. Ferguson was one of thousands of soldiers on both sides who died at the pivotal Civil War Battle of Gettysburg on July 1-3, 1863. That battle thwarted Confederate General Robert E. Lee's plan to take the war to the north. The battle is viewed by historians as a turning point, although the conflict wouldn't end until the spring of 1865.

Not many Beverly men fought at Gettysburg, since the 8th Massachusetts Regiment with its large local contingent wasn't there. But Ferguson had enlisted for three years in the First Massachusetts Regiment, which as part of the Army of the Potomac was in the thick of the conflict.

Charles F. Ferguson was born in Beverly December 8, 1838, the third of five children of William and Mary Ferguson. A mariner by trade, he came home from the sea in the spring of 1861 to learn that North and South were at war. Almost immediately he joined the First Massachusetts, enlisting in June and being mustered in August. In all he participated in 20 battles. Promoted to corporal on February 14, 1862, he was wounded for the first time at Fair Oaks, Virginia a few months later. After he recovered, he rejoined his regiment and was promoted to sergeant in November of 1862.

Ferguson was seriously wounded at Gettysburg and was treated at a military hospital near the battlefield. He lingered until September 11, 1863, dying just a few months short of his 25th birthday. His body was carried home to Beverly for a funeral on October 8th at First Baptist Church. Reverend Joseph Foster paid tribute to him as "a true soldier." Five local sergeants served as pallbearers as his body was conveyed to the cemetery, where the Beverly Light Infantry fired several volleys in tribute to a fallen comrade.

A version of this article appeared in the October 2014 e-newsletter of the Beverly Historical Society.

Women's Work in the Civil War
By Terri McFadden

The U.S. Sanitary Commission (USSC) was a civilian organization, formed during the Civil War, and the only such group authorized by President Lincoln. Their initial goal was to address the appalling lack of clean drinking water and the spread of disease in the army camps. Soon, however the lack of supplies and the need to provide assistance to the soldiers increased the scope of the Commission. Women all over the Union states became involved, including many in Beverly.

They gathered blankets and clothing, provided food, bandages and other supplies which were shipped to Boston for distribution. In the early days of the war many well-meaning efforts were wasted. Food arrived at the front lines rotting; bedding and clothes were ruined by weather. A serious effort was made to organize the USCC. Two Beverly women were leaders, organizing locally and statewide.

Hannah Rantoul (1821-1898), left, was the head of the Beverly branch of USCC and Anna Loring Dresel (1820-1896) served as Vice-President of the Boston chapter. Notices in the *Beverly Citizen* noted the many types of supplies sought by the women volunteering for the USSC, including "Cotton shirts, cotton drawers, towels and handkerchiefs, slippers…will be gratefully received and forwarded if sent to Miss Rantoul."

The Boston office was meticulous in their record keeping. The report for 1863-1864 notes that 11,190 soldiers received assistance. Help ranged from providing lodging, providing transportation for the wounded and men on leave, loaning money and securing employment for disabled soldiers. In that single year 16,351 meals were provided for soldiers in Boston alone. The female managers, like Anna Loring Dresel, worked with civic organizations and businesses to gather supplies. Money was raised in a variety of ways. Churches and school children gathered money, which they sent to Miss Rantoul. Town fairs were held to raise funds, which had the added benefit of raising community morale during the long years of brutal war.

The gratitude of the soldiers is obvious in the many letters they wrote to thank Miss Rantoul and her helpers. One Ohio man wrote to "The Ladies of Beverly" thanking them for "several articles of luxury" which included "…a gown, handkerchief, pin wheel, and soldier's prayer book." He noted that when he left the hospital in New Orleans he would leave the gown behind, but he would carry with him the little book and "cherish it as a sacred relic of this war."

Following the war, the organizing experience gained by many women involved in the work of the Sanitary Commission was put to another use – that of fighting for the right to vote.

A version of this article appeared in the September 2015 e-newsletter of the Beverly Historical Society.

A Soldier in the 55th

By Ed and Terri McFadden

Dotting Beverly's Central Cemetery are identical white headstones engraved with a name and military unit. These are the headstones of local men who served in America's Civil War (1861-1865). One stone is set slightly apart and on its own. It reads: "Geo. Stephens Company H 55th Mass Inf." For a time, this bit of information was all that we could learn about George Stephens. We guessed that George was a black man because the 55th Massachusetts Infantry formed at almost the same time as the more famous 54th and both were 'colored' regiments. Our research indicates that George Stevens – all the records except his headstone indicate this spelling – was the only black man from Beverly to serve in the Civil War.

George Stevens was born about 1850 in Shiloh, North Carolina. Both his death record and that of his mother, Martha, indicate that they were formerly enslaved. We know that George and his mother made their way to Beverly prior to July of 1864, when George enlisted. Whether or not they had escaped slavery is harder to prove. If they had, the

Fugitive Slave Act of 1850 would have required local citizens to assist in their arrest and return to slavery.

Both "Negro" regiments formed quickly when President Lincoln opened the army to men of color in 1863; black men were eager to serve. We know that George Stevens volunteered for the 54th Regiment, mustering on July 22, 1864 and he was transferred to the 55th in October. His enlistment papers indicate that he was 18 years old, but it is likely that he was just 14 or 15 – later records state he was born in 1850.

Soon afterward the 55th was sent to South Carolina where the regiment saw action on James Island and they were part of the force sent into Charleston in 1865. Private Stevens mustered out in Charleston and returned home to Beverly. He married Susie Cox of Lynn in 1877 and they had four children. George worked as a hostler, taking care of horses at a stable on Fayette Street. The Stevens home was just around the corner at 6 River Street.

Stevens died at age 56 in March of 1906. Questions about George Stevens abound. Had he escaped slavery? What was it like to be a formerly enslaved and a Union soldier in the south at in the last days of the Civil War? Were he and his family accepted in Beverly or were they shunned because of the color of their skin? It isn't really possible to answer these questions; however we can and do honor his service to the cause of union and liberty. A poem by Paul Lawrence Dunbar (1872-1906) called *The Colored Soldier* is a fitting tribute. It reads in part:

> *So all honor and all glory*
> *To those noble sons of Ham*
> *The gallant colored soldier*
> *Who fought for Uncle Sam!*

A version of this article appeared in August 2017 in the e-newsletter of the Beverly Historical Society.

The Not-so phony $3.00 Bill

By Edward R. Brown

Many people are familiar with the old expression "as phony as a three-dollar bill." But in the collection of Historic Beverly is a real three-dollar bill. A bill, which in its time, could be spent as legal tender hereabouts.

Before the 1860s individual banks were allowed to print their own currency. The Beverly Bank, established here in 1802, took advantage of that, hiring an engraver to design paper money, which was backed by gold kept in the bank vault. Our $3 bill dates from 1858. Paper money of this and other denominations, marked *Beverly Bank,* were accepted wherever the bank was known. The lack of a national currency attracted counterfeiters; some of this is also in the collection, perhaps it was recognized by the bank clerk and seized.

The confusion and problems caused by loose banking regulations were finally addressed, partly as a means to finance the Civil War. In 1863 Congress passed the National Currency Act and the National Banking Act a year later. Chartered National Banks now could issue standardized paper money in styles and denominations approved by the U.S. Comptroller of the Currency. The Beverly Bank applied for and obtained a federal charter, changing its name to Beverly National Bank. There would be no more $3 bills – except for in the Cabot House display case.

A version of this article appeared in the September 2014 e-newsletter of the Beverly Historical Society.

A Little Detective Work
By Terri McFadden

Windows into the past sometimes open unexpectedly. One Christmas I was given David McCullough's book *The Johnstown Flood*, - a real page-turner of a history book. I was nearly at the end of the book when I read "...there would be much speculation on how many of those people listed among the unfound dead were actually very much alive in some far-off place...eleven years later, in the summer of 1900, a man by the name of Leroy Temple showed up in town to confess that he had not died in the flood but had been living quite happily ever since in Beverly, Massachusetts." The jolt I received reading that sentence sent me on an historic quest. I had to know more of Leroy's story.

Leroy Temple was born in 1857 in Middlesex County, Massachusetts, one of five children of William and Ruth Temple. Sometime in the early 1880s he moved Johnstown, Pennsylvania a boomtown in the western part of the state. The steel-making business was in full flower, manufacturing metal for the expanding network of railroads. Leroy first worked as a laborer, but by 1889 he was a "cupola liner" - making liners for vertical furnaces which were used to melt iron prior to casting.

On May 31, 1889 the disaster that many had feared for years, happened. The South Fork dam burst, and thousands of people and animals were swept along the narrow valley by a 40-foot wall of water along with locomotives and train cars, hundreds of buildings and whole hillsides of trees. More than 2,200 of the dead were identified and 750 more were unknown. Others were simply listed as missing.

Leroy Temple was one of many who were trapped at the Pennsylvania Railroad's massive stone bridge, where the mountain of debris was stopped. The bridge kept more damage from occurring downriver. But many victims were trapped in the rubble and either drowned or burned to death when the huge pile caught fire. Even with the frantic help of rescue workers, many victims were unable to escape. On the morning of June 1st Leroy Temple was one of the lucky ones when he was freed. McCullough writes that Temple "...looked at the remains of Johnstown, then turned on his heels and walked right out of the valley."

By 1893 Leroy was living in Beverly, but now he had a wife and five stepchildren. His new wife was named Viola, a widow who had lived in Johnstown following her first marriage to Frederick Schade in 1875. The couple had one son and four daughters and lived on Market Street in downtown Johnstown, where Frederick made and sold cigars for a living. He died in 1885 and where Viola lived for the next four years is unclear. Perhaps she moved back to Bellefonte, Pennsylvania where she was born and still had family.

Following their marriage in 1890 Leroy and Viola moved to Beverly. They rented various homes in the city, living on Balch Street, School Street and Pleasant Street. Leroy was a "teamster" or "jobber" first hauling ice to customers in Beverly. Later he specialized in moving furniture and pianos and "expressing of all kinds."

Leroy Temple died in 1912 and Viola stayed in Beverly for a time, then moved back to Bellefonte. Later she lived with her daughter Edith in Cambridge. After her death in 1924 she was buried in the North Beverly Cemetery.

Historical research sometimes adds more questions than it answers. Some of the details of Leroy and Viola's journey remain unknown. Did they know each other in Johnstown? Did Leroy turn to the widowed Viola for help after the disastrous flood? Why did they choose to move to Beverly? Like any good mystery more clues may someday help to put the rest of the pieces together. However, it is comforting to know that Beverly provided a safe haven for a survivor of one of America's worst disasters.

A version of this article was printed in the Spring 2015 issue of the *Chronicle*.

Gardening for Victory

By Gail Balentine

This 1942 manual advised how to nurture plentiful and profitable gardens.

Victory Gardens began during World War I to help feed the troops by reducing the demand for vegetables at home. Reinstituted during World War II, an estimated 20 million Victory Gardens were planted in sites that ranged from flowerpots to large public tracts. These "Sunday Farmers" produced more than eight million tons of food that was either eaten fresh—"meatless Mondays" were encouraged—or processed and preserved for the winter.

Eleanor Roosevelt had a Victory Garden planted on the White House lawn, and familiar places such as Alcatraz, Ellis Island, Copley Square, the Boston Common, and the Public Garden all became food-producing sites. In May of 1943, *Life Magazine* called gardening for the war effort" . . . the greatest outdoor fad since miniature golf."

Beverly citizens were no exception, joining the rest of the nation in producing food. On April 13, 1943, it was estimated that Beverly had more than 1,000 Victory Gardens, including land at the United Shoe Machine Corporation that was set aside for employees to plant their gardens. Local citizens were aided in their efforts by a column published in the *Beverly Evening Times*, by publications from the Beverly Victory Garden Committee, and through public lectures held at the Briscoe School by Essex Aggie, the local agricultural school. The Seed Store at 70 Park Street sold a Victory Garden seed package containing 14 varieties for $1.00, among them beans, beets, spinach, and Swiss chard. Planting, tending, and harvesting fruits and vegetables became morale boosters and one way for those at home to feel as if they were doing their part for the war effort.

A version of this article appeared in the May 2015 e-newsletter of the Beverly Historical Society.

What are YOU doing?

By Gail Balentine

During World Wars I and II, the government encouraged Americans to grow their own food to free up commercially grown crops to feed military personnel and our allies. People across the country embraced the concept and the home-front effort became a way for civilians to help defeat the enemy. In order to extend the bounty beyond the growing season, home food processing using either water baths or pressure cookers was the next step.

The Beverly Victory Garden Committee sponsored classes in canning and the local newspaper published information for those new to the process, as did national radio stations. Advice was given on how to assure proper canning temperatures, sterilize containers, and create an effective seal on canning jars. A national poll conducted in January 1944 found that 75% of U.S. housewives canned some of the produce they grew; the average was 165 jars per year.

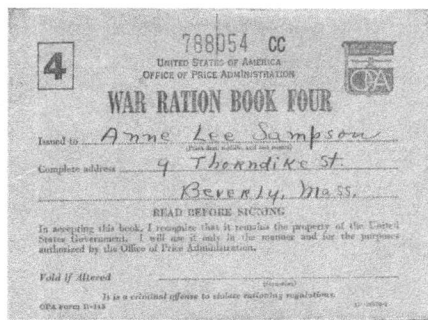

This 1943 ration book owned by Anne L. Sampson, contained stamps that were redeemable for rationed goods.

Even after the war copies of the classic American guide to food preservation, the Ball Blue Book of Preserving, remained in family kitchens like ours. My mother continued canning vegetables for many years after the war. In fact, I was a teenager before I realized that not everyone could just run down to the cellar and grab a jar or two of tomatoes when they needed them!

A version of this article appeared in the September 2015 e-newsletter of the Beverly Historical Society.

Civilian Defense: Ready for Action!

By Gail Balentine and Terri McFadden

Even before bombs were dropped on Pearl Harbor, American citizens prepared for what seemed to be the inevitability of war. In May 1941 the Aircraft Warning Service (AWS) was formed as a civilian branch of the Army Ground Observer Corps, under the command of the Army Air Force. Following the attack on December 7, 1941, many people who couldn't join the military were recruited to the AWS. All observers received training in aircraft recognition and thousands of observation posts were established. At its peak the AWS on the east coast had 750,000 people in its service.

During the winter of 1940-1941 the Beverly post of the American Legion began planning the 24 hour-a-day airplane alert system that was put into effect at 4:00 pm on December 8, 1941. One hundred and thirty volunteers, on rotating duty, reported suspicious aircraft. Three deputy chief wardens and seven precinct wardens reported to Chief Warden R. Leveret Murray to keep the system running smoothly. Even students from Beverly High were recruited as assistant wardens. On March 4, 1942, the Beverly post was commended for its work by the War Department. Training sessions for AWS volunteers and nursing volunteers were offered and residents who owned cars were sought to serve as evacuation volunteers. The public works department offered "Air Raid Sand" to Beverly residents to combat incendiary bombs. In addition to ground spotters a Civil Air Patrol was organized, consisting of 65 private, commercial and student pilots. This group helped patrol the local Atlantic coast looking for German submarines. It is one of the few surviving WWII civil defense organizations.

In May of 1944, the federal government decided that the acute need for civil defense was past and the Aircraft Warning Service was disbanded. Other wartime efforts were also abandoned as the war ended. Beverly citizens, like thousands across the nation, had worked diligently to keep their homes safe from an enemy attack, which thankfully never came.

A version of this article appeared in the November 2015 e-newsletter of the Beverly Historical Society.

Beverly and the Atomic Bomb
By Edward R. Brown

Hard though it may be for people today to believe, Beverly played a key role in both of the atomic bomb missions of August 1945 against Japan. These terrible bombs convinced Emperor Hirohito to overrule his military planners and end World War II by accepting unconditional surrender. Use of atomic weapons, along with the entry of the Russians into the Asian war, avoided the incredible bloodshed that would have accompanied the military invasion of Japan planned for November 1945. Those missions, authorized by President Harry S. Truman and flown by crews of the Army Air Corp's top secret 509th Composite Group based on Tinian Island, destroyed the city of Hiroshima and flattened the industrial zone of Nagasaki. The first mission used America's only uranium bomb while the second employed a plutonium "Fat Man" device.

The "bullet" mechanism that set off the explosion 1800 feet above Hiroshima on August 6 was developed at the Metal Hydrides plant on Congress Street in Beverly – the company later known as Ventron and Morton Thiokol. Metal Hydrides (aerial view left) came to Beverly in 1940. It was headed by Peter Alexander, who had invented a way to produce rare metals using hydrides, chemical com-pounds containing hydrogen. In 1942, the United States launched the expensive and highly classified Manhattan Project to develop an atomic bomb, after President Franklin Roosevelt learned that Nazi Germany was engaged in a similar pursuit. Top secret locations were set up, and Alexander's company was employed to do secret work involving highly toxic uranium. The location was the site of a federal Department of Energy radiation cleanup in 1999.

Workers at Metal Hydrides found themselves doing strange and ultimately hazardous duties they didn't understand. Some of the results were shipped to the University of Chicago, where physicists working underground first proved that nuclear fission was attainable. One Metal Hydrides employee, Carney Taylor, recalled in later years asking Alexander what it was they were doing, and the boss replied that "a piece of metal the size of a walnut could take a ship across the ocean." A piece of uranium about that size would fire down the barrel of the Hiroshima bomb to trigger the nuclear explosion.

The Nagasaki mission had a different local connection. The "weaponeer" in charge of the 'Fat Man' bomb aboard the B-29 "Bock's Car" on August 9th was Navy Commander Frederick L. "Dick" Ashworth, a 1928 graduate of Beverly High School, where he was student council president and a member of the track team. A decorated Navy combat pilot in the Pacific campaign, Ashworth was recruited into the Manhattan Project in 1944 by a key player at the Los Alamos, New Mexico research base, Navy Captain William S. "Deak" Parsons, the two would be the only "weaponeers" authorized to fly atomic combat missions. Parsons accompanied Colonial Paul Tibbets aboard the B-29 "Enola Gay" on the Hiroshima mission.

While that mission went perfectly, Ashworth, pilot Major Chuck Sweeney of Quincy, Massachusetts and their crew experienced a harrowing trip. Finding their primary target, Kokura, socked in with smoke and haze, they diverted to the secondary, Nagasaki, only to find conditions no better there. Under orders to make a visual drop only, Ashworth had authorized a desperation radar drop when bombardier Kermit Beahan found a hole in the clouds and let the weapon go visually. At the same moment the pilot executed a 155-degree dive turn to get the plane clear of the explosion. With fuel running out, Sweeney then brought the B-29 to an emergency landing on the recently captured island of Okinawa, saving the lives of the 12 men on board. After the war, it was Ashworth who chose the Bikini atoll as the site for the 1946

U.S. atomic bomb tests. Despite the death toll from the bombings, Ashworth, like all the other crew members of the "Enola Gay," "Bock's Car" and the "Great Artiste" - which carried the scientific measuring instruments on both missions – harbored no guilt feelings after the war. By ending the war, despite the terrible new weapons unleashed, they averted the carnage for both sides that would have resulted from an invasion of the Japanese homeland.

A version of this article appeared in the Winter 2006 issue of the *Chronicle*.

Just Another Boy from Beverly
By Terri McFadden

It isn't often that I have seen a group of objects that tell a story that is charming, informative and tragic, but this is a fair description of the collection of John D. Roger (1912-1956). This small group of objects consists of military photographs and memorabilia from World War II and the decade afterward.

Rogers was born on October 10, 1912, the eldest child of James and Mary Rogers who raised their nine children in various locations in Beverly. James supported his large family working in a shoemaking factory and later as a gardener. The children attended local schools and John graduated from Beverly High. In 1938 he married Lucy Primmer in Maine and the couple settled in Beverly. John followed his father's occupation at first, earning his living as a landscape gardener on one of the large estates in town.

As it did so many others, the entry of the United States into World War II caused a major change in John Roger's life. He joined the army on

June 6, 1942 and became a member of the Army Air Corps. His marriage did not survive and he and Lucy divorced "under friendly terms" according to a relative. After the war he continued in the military and served in the Air Force after it became a separate branch in 1947. Most of his years of service were at foreign posts; he truly saw the world. Italy, Germany, China, India and Africa were just a few of the places he was assigned.

Objects in the collection give a glimpse of military life in the '40s and '50s. They include an Army Air Force Technical School graduation program, a three-day pass dated 1944, a berthing card for the *S.S. Orduna*, a copy of a message from General Douglas MacArthur to the Emperor of Japan, and a ticket for 1 beer at "Joes Joint" – apparently unredeemed. Several unsigned sketches show amusing scenes of army life. If they were drawn by John Rogers, he was a talented cartoonist.

Finally, in 1956 after nearly 14 years in the service, John Rogers decided to retire. He came home to Beverly for one week and as a last duty went to California to deliver secret documents for the military. Three days after his arrival John was walking in the base parking lot when he was struck by a car driven by a drunken 21-year-old soldier. The impact threw him fifteen feet into the air and he was killed instantly. Virginia Rogers, the relative who donated the collection to the Beverly Historical Society wrote that "John loved life – the Air Force and most of all his country. He was no hero, just another boy from Beverly."

A version of this article appeared in the October 2016 e-newsletter of the Beverly Historical Society.

Chapter 3: Getting Around

The Carriage Man
By Terri McFadden

In the fall of 2014 a small memento of Beverly's business history came to light in the back yard of Cabot House. A small metal label, inscribed "R.C. BRUHM Beverly Mass", was found under the beech tree. This label was once affixed to a carriage or sleigh and proclaimed the business of Robert C. Bruhm, which stood at 14 ½ Roundy Street. The self-described "Carriage Man", Robert Bruhm was a carriage dealer, maker, repairer and painter. He had emigrated from Canada in 1890 and established his business here a few years later. One of Bruhm's vehicles, a carriage which can be converted to a sleigh, is in the collection of Historic Beverly. It is just one of many types of carriages made by Bruhm's small company.

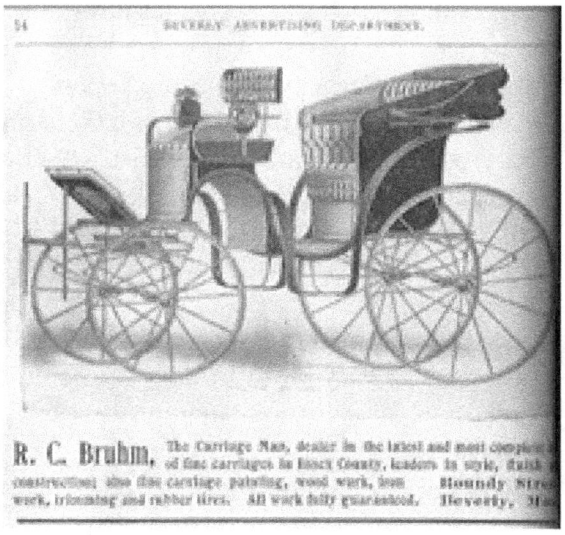

The proliferation of automobiles in the early 20th century brought an end to the ancient skill of carriage making. By 1920 the Bruhm realized that his trade was on its way out. He managed to make the transition to the modern world, doing auto body work and painting – useful certainly, but somehow lacking in the romance of the Carriage Man and his vehicles.

A version of the article was printed in the January 2015 e-newsletter of the Beverly Historical Society.

Railroad Hotels

By Edward R. Brown

In 1897, the Boston and Maine Railroad built a new depot in Beverly with a design by the award-winning architect Bradford Lee Gilbert. The main building survives as the Beverly Depot Restaurant and the station continues to serve 1,000 or more commuters on a typical weekday. Along with the upgraded facilities came railroad hotels to serve visitors coming to town as well as railroad employees stopping over. The Naumkeag Directory for 1897-98 featured display ads for three hotels located nearby.

Perhaps the most prominent was the Hotel Walter, named for its proprietor Horace A. Walter. Located at 80-82 Rantoul Street at the corner of Railroad Avenue, the Walter described itself as a "first class family and transient hotel." Rooms on the second and third floors could be rented by the day or week at "popular prices." The hotel was "modern in all its appointments, and two minutes' walk to the depot." For those who wanted to travel or go exploring about the city, "electrics" – meaning street cars – passed by the door. An "elegant' coffee shop and lunch room were connected on the ground floor, with "cuisine unsurpassed."

The Park and Trafton Hotels were constructed near Beverly Depot for railroad travelers.

Nearby at the corner of Park Street and Railroad Avenue stood the Hotel Trafton, whose proprietor was Darling L. Trafton. With verandas surrounding both its first and second stories, the Trafton described itself as a "first class commercial hotel." Rooms were available on both the European and American plans, with the latter costing $2 a day. A short distance away and a bit less elegant was The Boscobel at 43 Bow St., which was not ashamed to call itself a boarding house. The proprietor was Mrs. Annie Wardman. The Boscobel offered board and rooms by the day or week at "terms reasonable." Mrs. Wardman advertised that her premises offered both steam heat and bathrooms. All of these establishments thrived as the traveling public took advantage of the ease of railroad travel.

A version of this article appeared in the June 2015 e-newsletter of the Beverly Historical Society.

When Mr. Frick Arrived in Style
By Edward R. Brown

It was in 1906 when steel magnate Henry Clay Frick, one of America's wealthiest industrialists, erected his palatial summer mansion, Eagle Rock, on the Prides Crossing shoreline. With its ornate fences along Hale Street and stables on the inland side that rivaled many a mansion in their scope, Eagle Rock was perhaps the jewel of the Gold Coast era.

Frick and his wife, Adelaide, would arrive for the season from Pittsburgh or New York via special railroad accommodations. Since railroad stock comprised a large segment of his considerable investment portfolio, this wasn't a difficult matter to arrange. His leased palaces on wheels included the private Pullman *Commonwealth*, in which the Fricks arrived in May of 1910 along with three other cars which contained the family luggage, his automobiles and a portion of his world-renowned art collection. But that same year he ordered from the Pullman Company a piece of rolling stock that would be the ultimate in traveling luxury. Frick called his luxurious car *Westmoreland* after the Pennsylvania county where he had been born.

It was aboard *Westmoreland* that Mr. and Mrs. Frick and their daughter Helen, made their way east on the Gloucester Branch tracks behind a Boston & Maine locomotive in June of 1911. A correspondent for the *North Shore Breeze*, a magazine which reported on the local social scene, was allowed a brief glimpse of the interior. Equipped with three bedrooms, the walls were upholstered in satin tapestry of green, red and pink, each with an adjoining bath. A living room, dining room and kitchenette completed the accommodations - all the luxuries that wealth and privilege demanded. Even the silverware and china had been created especially for the car and bore the *Westmoreland* emblem.

Such a magnificent piece of railroad glory could not of course be entrusted to a siding in some rail yard. Mr. Frick's personal car had its own stuccoed, window-less house beside the tracks not far from the Prides Crossing depot, with a spur track leading to it. That structure would outlast the car it was built to house. Mr. Frick only enjoyed the use of *Westmoreland* for nine seasons before dying in December of 1919. Adelaide Frick continued to summer at Eagle Rock until her death in 1931. She gave the elegant car to a family friend and willed that after his death the car be destroyed. *Westmoreland* met its end in 1967 and Eagle Rock was demolished in the early 1970s. As for the shed constructed to house *Westmoreland*, it kept a lonely vigil beside the tracks until 1967, when it was replaced by a private home.

A version of this article appeared in the May 2016 e-newsletter of the Beverly Historical Society.

Frick's luxurious car Westmoreland

Goodbye Water Tank

By Edward R. Brown

For more than 45 years, it stood sentinel, a landmark on River Street just beyond the Beverly Depot platform. Erected in 1907 by the Boston & Maine Railroad, the 50,000-gallon water tank catered to the needs of a long line of steam locomotives that worked in or passed through Beverly. These included the 0-6-0 switchers shuttling cars in what was once an extensive Beverly freight yard. Timetables also showed a few Mogul or Pacific-drawn local passenger trains that came out of North Station, turned on the Beverly turntable, and returned to Boston after filling their water cisterns. Every now and then a through train stopping at Beverly might need a quick drink. The water tank was filled automatically via a two-inch city line from River Street, and a spout could be lowered by the train crew reach the cistern on the locomotive tender.

In 1953, former city of Beverly Public Works Commissioner, James Blackmer, recalled for the local press that the erection of the tank in 1907 came as a result of city complaints to the B&M. Before that year, railroad firemen wishing to water their steamy steeds used a spigot directly attached to the municipal water line. When the spigot was activated, the sudden change in water pressure produced a "hammer" in the cement pipe then in use, sometimes resulting in a break.

Changing technology eventually made the tank obsolete. By the 1950s diesel power had taken over the freight work and all but a couple of the passenger trains. On March 26, 1953 a B&M maintenance crew headed by foreman Harold Eldridge arrived in town with specific orders. The last of the water was drained from the tank, police shut down River Street for safety reasons and the demolition crew proceeded with a carefully worked out plan. Men first cut about three-quarters of the way through the eight supports that held up the tank. Cables were then attached to the supports and after a crane took hold of the cables, the tank was gracefully toppled onto River Street, landing within two feet of the calculated spot. With the tank in pieces on the ground, workers with torches cut up the debris. It was hauled of town, not on railroad

The Water Tower is on the left

cars, but on flatbed trucks, leaving nothing to mark where a relic of the days of steam locomotives had once stood.

A version of this article appeared in the Fall 2015 issue of the *Chronicle*.

Sunday Newspaper Trains: Unseen & Vital
By Edward R. Brown

Of all the first-class trains that visited Beverly and nearby towns, the most anonymous were the Sunday morning newspaper trains operated by the Boston & Maine from the 1930s to the 1950s. Running in the hours of darkness, they were rarely photographed and seldom seen. Those trains out of Boston ran to most major points on the B&M system. They were loaded at "A House" on the Lechmere side of the North Station yards. Sunday readers had the choice of the *Boston Globe*, *Herald*, *Post*, *Monitor*, and *Record*.

Beverly had two Sunday paper trains, 2001 to Portsmouth and 2551 to Rockport. Those trains weren't in the public timetable, only in the employee timetable, but the latter did not restrict them as "X" trains, meaning no passengers allowed. So, railroad employees and other off-hours riders who knew about them could board and alight.

Both the 2001 and 2551 left Boston as one, at 3:30 am, the last to depart, combined and double-headed, with two of the B&M's 4-6-2 steam locomotives at the head. The Gloucester Branch engine was in the lead. On arrival at Salem about 4:07 they were divided. Both trains included passenger coaches needed for the return trips. The lead engine was unpinned and seems to have run light through the old Salem Tunnel to clear onto the Danvers branch track. After a brakeman pulled the pin to separate the Portsmouth cars from the Rockport ones, number 2001 got rolling again at 4:13. After a brief stop at Beverly it headed north, calling on all stations along the way, arriving in Portsmouth at 5:42.

Men who worked the Sunday newspaper trains worked out of cars like these.

With the Portsmouth train gone the first engine reversed through the tunnel, negotiated the spring switch, and backed onto its cars, creating the 2551 for a 4:31 departure from Salem. That this train carried the Beverly paper bundles is shown by the seven-minute stop it was allocated at Beverly depot. It then entered the branch, stopping at Beverly Farms, Manchester and Gloucester, arriving in Rockport at 5:34.

Number 2551 was the first to disappear, at the end of April in 1953, when trucks began bringing the Sunday news to Cape Ann. The 2001 held on until 1957, with a 1500 series diesel taking over from the scrapped steamer. Then all of the business went to trucks. The newspaper trains were remembered only by the crews who once worked on them, and the sleepy couriers who unloaded them and delivered the Sunday papers to local newsstands.

A version of this article appeared in the Spring 2015 issue of the *Chronicle*.

The Three Beverly Depots
By Edward R. Brown

The Eastern Railroad, chartered in 1836, opened its line from East Boston to Salem in August of 1838, using four Lowell-built 0-4-0 wood burner locomotives named *Suffolk, Essex, Merrimack* and *Rockingham,* as was the fashion of the time. The journey took only about 45  minutes – compared to more than two hours by stage. The speed and the six daily trips soon put the stagecoach out of business, although inbound passengers had to complete their journey by boarding a ferry to Boston. A year later the first Eastern train rolled into Beverly on a trestle bridge across the Danvers River. The line was soon pushed north through Wenham, Hamilton, Ipswich, Rowley and Newburyport and on to New Hampshire and Maine.

Beverly riders first boarded at a small wooden station located just across the bridge near the present Congress Street crossing (above). In 1854 things became much more convenient for Beverly residents when the second station was erected much nearer to the downtown, at Park Street. That same year Eastern did away with the ferry by using the former Grand Junction Railroad through North Chelsea (now Revere) and on to a new Boston Terminal near Haymarket Square.

The second Beverly depot offered (below, demolished 1896) many more amenities than the primitive original, and by 1868 Beverly had ten passenger trains each way to and from Boston. In 1873 they had grown to 14, and there were even a couple express trains to the big city. The first station master was Joseph Henry Herrick, born in 1812. He had first been hired by the Eastern Railroad in 1847; his job was to line the switch for the four Gloucester Branch passenger trains and one local freight. After seven years of probably boring, though essential work, Mr. Herrick was rewarded with promotion to station master.

Beverly had extensive sidings and freight yards by 1880. An interesting feature of the second passenger depot was that it boasted three tracks, with a middle iron between the inbound and outbound platforms. That permitted a dangerous and highly unorthodox procedure on the 12:15 pm train out of Boston, which would horrify officials today. Francis B.C. Bradlee, who wrote an extensive history of the Eastern Railroad, described the scene: "The noon train for Portland for years hauled the Gloucester Branch cars as far as Beverly. Behind the latter were spare cars also to be left at Beverly. When the other end of the Beverly bridge was reached, and while the train was in motion, the Gloucester cars were uncoupled and the locomotive and the Portland cars would steam ahead and come into Beverly on the outward track. The switch would then be quickly changed and the Gloucester train would roll in on its own momentum on the middle track where a locomotive would be waiting to take it to Rockport. In the mean-time the spare cars were separated from those to Gloucester, the switch again thrown, and they would come in on the inbound track."

Designed by prominent New York architect, Bradford Lee Gilbert, the third depot opened in 1897. Today, it looks much the same as it did 100 years ago. In 1965 the ticket office closed and the railroad sold the building not long after-ward. After a fire in February 1971 the depot was renovated and reopened as restaurant in December. More than 2000 riders board at Beverly Depot on a typical weekday, the third highest number inbound riders on the line after Salem and Providence.

A version of this article was published in the Fall 2012 issue of the *Chronicle*.

The Wreck at Prides Crossing
By Edward R. Brown

On August 11, 1981, a disastrous train wreck occurred on the Gloucester Branch just west of the little used Pride's Crossing station, a wreck that given modern dispatching methods seemed impossible.

On that day the inbound track was closed for repairs, meaning that Boston-bound passenger trains had to use the outbound track between Manchester and Beverly Junction. The late afternoon Train 570, which originated in Gloucester instead of Rockport, and carrying a number of summer day trippers, had been cleared at Manchester to cross over as usual at Beverly Farms. Extra freight 1731 East from Salem to Gloucester never should have been allowed to enter the branch until after the 570 had cleared, and as an extra with no regular schedule had to operate on train orders. Yet someone really dropped the ball, and the two trains smashed head-on just east of a sharp curve near the west Thissell Street crossing.

Paul Sullivan of Rockport, a veteran engineer just days away from retirement, was in the cab of control coach #1301, which led Train 570, fortunately empty of riders. "Sully" went into the crash blowing his whistle to warn his passengers and crew. He was killed instantly. The engineer and conductor of the freight train jumped, just in time, but the brakeman and an unauthorized rider in the cab died. About 20 passengers and the assistant conductor of the passenger train were injured.

After the investigation, a dispatcher reportedly was fired, but the damage was done and lives forever altered.

A version of this article appeared in the August 2014 e-newsletter of the Beverly Historical Society.

Prides Crossing Depot

By Edward R. Brown

In 1879 the Eastern Railroad erected a new depot on Hale Street, where the road crossed what was then a single-track Gloucester Branch line. The railroad named it Prides Crossing after the Pride family that had lived in the vicinity for several generations.

Prides soon became an important stop for the rich and famous Gold Coast residents who made the area their summer playground from the late 19th century and into the early 20th. Henry Clay Frick, owner of the Eagle Rock estate, even had a large car shed beside the tracks to house his private Pullman.

In its heyday Prides Crossing had its own station agent and baggage master. But by the 1930s the glory years were coming to an end. After World War II more and more passenger trains began to bypass Prides, and today only a few weekday rush hour trains still stop there for the convenience of a dozen or so commuters. The station has retained much of its original appearance and now, recently repainted, it houses a popular candy store.

A version of this article appeared in the October 2015 e-newsletter of the Beverly Historical Society.

Montserrat Station

By Edward R. Brown

First opened in the 1890s as a flag stop station, the Montserrat depot on Essex Street assumed new importance when President William Howard Taft chose Beverly as his "summer White House." Taft's special train from Washington arrived "wrong iron" at Montserrat on July 4, 1909, where the Tafts alighted to make their way to the Evan's Estate, at today's Lynch Park. Conversion of the former Peabody's Field baseball park nearby into a housing development gave fresh impetus to the first stop on the Gloucester Branch. The photo, taken circa 1910, shows the vine-covered depot in its glory days. Compare that to its decrepit, unsafe appearance on May 23, 1964, when the deteriorating Boston & Maine stopped there at the risk of riders.

In 1958, the B&M sold nearly all of its station buildings to eliminate property taxes and save maintenance costs. The buyer of Montserrat station hoped to convert it to a store, but after a long dispute with the city over zoning, gave up and left the building to rot. Since the railroad no longer owned the property, it ignored pleas from the city to do something. On the night of March 19, 1966, the depot was destroyed by fire. For nearly 20 years railroad patrons had only a crumbling, uncovered platform to mark the stop.

When the drawbridge between Beverly and Salem burned in 1984, shutting down train service for a year, the MBTA constructed new platforms on both tracks along with a shelter for inbound riders. Today a dozen weekday trains each way serve Montserrat, during rush hour and mostly flag stops on the off-hours. Where the station building once stood is now a parking lot for commuters.

A version of this article appeared in the Winter 2014 Chronicle.

A Fiery Detour
By Edward R. Brown

The morning of Friday, November 16, 1984, started out normally for North Shore commuters taking the trains starting from Rockport and Ipswich. But their return home for the weekend would be problematic at best.

About mid-afternoon, fire departments in Beverly and Salem began to receive reports of smoke coming from the wooden trestle bridge that carried railroad tracks between the two cities. Within minutes, flames were licking at the pilings and soon the bridge was a mass of flames from end to end, defying the efforts of frustrated firefighters. When the spectacular blaze finally burned itself out, this vital link on the transportation system was nothing but a mass of twisted rails and charred pilings. Before the evening rush hour, Salem's Michaud Bus Company had marshalled as many buses and drivers as were available to meet the outbound trains at Salem and transport riders to Beverly and beyond.

The fire trapped two train sets north and east of the bridge. For a few weeks these were utilized to make shuttle runs between Rockport and Beverly depot, where buses continued to convey passengers to and from Salem. But maintaining those isolated engines and coaches became too difficult, and early in January the shuttle service was terminated. To get the trains back to Boston, they were first moved to Hamilton-Wenham station, where the engines and cars were separated and lifted, one by one with cranes, onto huge flat-bed trucks for the road trip to Boston.

To make things even more dicey for commuters a second fire had damaged the draw span outside of North Station, forcing another detour. Until repairs were completed, the MBTA was had to set up a temporary tent facility in the Charlestown yard. Passengers had to get off, walk to nearby Sullivan Square station and board an Orange Line train into the city. The once-easy commute to Boston had taken on the complexity of an international journey.

By January 1985, the "T" had worked out a $1million contract with Michaud Bus Company to supply buses to connect with all the trains at Salem. The Michaud brothers, "Gig" and "Spike" purchased 11 used deluxe coaches for the longer runs to Route 128, Rockport, Gloucester, Montserrat and Beverly Farms. Four school buses were used for the short haul to and from Beverly Depot. It worked as well as could be hoped for. "Short" riders, who traveled between stations on the branch lines, were simply out of luck. One change resulting from the fire was the permanent end to all revenue freight train service north and east of Salem. With their service cut off, the few remaining freight customers in Beverly, Gloucester and Newburyport had no choice other than to switch their business to trucking firms, and they never returned to the railroad.

A year would pass before the replacement bridge could be built and normal train service resumed. To get the work done the MBTA signed a $7.5 million contract with J.M. Cashman Inc. of Weymouth. Cashman crews got to work demolishing the destroyed bridge and building a new one, using reinforced concrete pilings in place of the ancient wooden ones. Unfortunately, funds weren't available to replace the elderly draw span that opened for boat traffic, so the old one was reinstalled. On November 19th, a year and three days after the fire, a test train made a first run over the new bridge, helping to settle the rails in place.

A special inaugural run was booked for November 29th, for all the dignitaries who could fit aboard the four coaches. It made a special stop at Chelsea so that Governor Michael S. Dukakis could formally dedicate the resumption of commuter rail service to that city; no trains had stopped there since 1958.

To the relief of those long-suffering commuters a new timetable was issued effective December 1, 1985, which restored 12 weekday trains to Rockport and 11 to Ipswich, all stopping at Beverly. The detour was officially over.

A version of this article appeared in the Fall 2017 issue of the *Chronicle*.

Chapter 4: Public Life

The Omnibus

By Edward R. Brown

In 1906 children attending the Bass River School –later called the Brown School – on Conant Street, got to school on this horse-drawn "omnibus." Seen in the photograph is little Hazel Dodge, her white skirt blowing in the breeze, climbing aboard to join her friends. Hazel, the daughter of market gardener Frederick and Nettie Dodge, lived at 203 Dodge Street. Bass River had five classrooms with 178 pupils divided unequally between grades 1 through 8. The first-grade class had 36 children but in grade 8 there were only 8 students. In the early 20th century many young people began their working life before completing the 8th grade.

Because of the far-flung homes in North Beverly, Bass River was the only elementary school to enjoy bus service in 1906. The other 11 schools were within walking distance for everyone. Records of the city auditor show that John W. Lovett was paid $600 that year for "transporting scholars to and from Bass River School," while for Stephen A. Gwinn received $288 for providing the same service. Being a school bus driver was a part-time job for both men.

From Oats to Octane
By Edward R. Brown

In the early years of the 20th century all apparatus used by the Beverly Fire Department was horse-drawn. It was an all-call department, with firemen assigned to companies and paid only when they turned out; even the chief was part-time at $325 a year. The only full-timer was in charge of caring for the animals and equipment.

The *Saturday Morning Citizen* of March 9, 1912 reported that Beverly "has made a step to purchase a motor fire truck." This would be economical, since "horses cost money and the kind that a city purchases a lot of money." Motor fire trucks had drawn praise elsewhere, and the editor predicted that never again would the city purchase a horse drawn vehicle.

Beverly's new steam pumper is being tested in 1892.

At the time Beverly owned three steam pumpers, two at Central Station and one at Beverly Farms, a ladder truck at Central with a smaller one at the Farms, and hose wagons in North Beverly, Centerville and on Rantoul Street at both School and Roundy. A department history compiled by the late Deputy Chief Robert May reveals that when the first motor truck built by American LaFrance was put in service December 16, 1912 it went not to headquarters but to replace Hose 2 at Rantoul and Roundy streets. That building later became the union hall for USM's UE Local 271 and is now (2015) the River House homeless shelter.

The next purchase was not a complete truck but a motor tractor to pull Engine 3 at Beverly Farms. There was a reason for this. Since the city did not supply horses for the Farms, the crew by arrangement had to borrow a team from a nearby stable when the alarm sounded. A similar three-wheel tractor, built by Knox-Martin, was acquired in 1914 to pull Ladder 1. On February 22, 1915 Central station got a new Combination 1, built by White-Kress.

In 1918 the mayor and city council bit the financial bullet, purchasing six motorized fire trucks, mostly from White-Kress, and three more acquisitions in early 1919 led to May's note on March 7: "Department motorized." The *Beverly Citizen* editor's 1912 prediction had been fulfilled. Gasoline replaced oats and hay in the budget. Full-time firefighters would now be needed. In 1919 Chief Robert H. Grant was full time at $1300 a year, and "engineers" (probably meaning engine drivers) Simeon Allen at Central and Walter "Soapo" Wright at the Farms were collecting $3.50 a day. But it wasn't until the mid-1960s that the last of the call men were retired from the roster and first alarms no longer had to be sounded on the fire horns.

 A version of this article appeared in the September 2015 e-newsletter of the Beverly Historical Society.

Enforcing the Law

By Terri McFadden

From the earliest days of the colony, Massachusetts lawmakers tried to ensure that citizens obeyed the law – and indeed that was a period when there were many laws which needed to be enforced. In each community men were chosen to be constables and they were given wide responsibilities. Among them were to collect taxes, deliver warrants, "to whip or punish anyone to be punished" - unless they could find someone else to take on that duty. Constables also could raise the "hue and cry" or pursue people accused of murder, theft and other major crimes. He was charged with arresting those who "broke the Sabbath," swore or got drunk, or were believed to be "vagrants or nightwalkers." Constables were also called on to stop domestic disputes. By law all men between 16 and 60 had to register to serve in the town watch and the constable was required to gather the names and submit them to authorities. As a symbol of his office the constable carried a black staff of five to five and half feet long and tipped with five or six inches of brass.

When Beverly parted ways with Salem and became a separate community in 1668, John Hill was serving as the constable and it was voted that he stay in the post for the remainder of his term. The next year Robert Hibbard, Sr. took over the job. It isn't clear where those accused of a crime in Beverly were sent in these early years. Later, however the local workhouse was used to incarcerate those picked up for drunkenness or disorderly conduct. These people served time without any trial if two Overseers of the Poor agreed to the charges. The Supreme Judicial Court declared this practice illegal in 1821. The town board of selectmen began to appoint an Inspector of Police in 1805 who was required to patrol the town "from time to time" and report at their monthly meetings. For most of the 19th century the police were considered "town officers" and not a separate department. It wasn't until 1874 that the Chief of Police position was created and the first police station constructed. Either the police chief position didn't require all his time or perhaps the pay wasn't enough to cover the bills, but William Moses, Beverly's first Chief of Police, in addition to enforcing the law, was also the town's lamplighter, lighting the gas lights that illuminated Beverly's main streets. Somehow that seems a step down from being the holder of the constable's staff of office!

The black staff of office was an important 17th century, symbol of the authority of the king. The black staff was carried by constables when executing court business. Made of white oak, this staff was carried by Andrew Elliot "who was allowed clerk of the writs for Beverly" in November 1678, was listed as constable in 1684, and was elected first town clerk of Beverly on April 11, 1690. Elliot was later named to the jury of the Salem Witchcraft Court of Oyer and Terminer. At a much later date the flag of England was overpainted with an American flag.

A version of this article appeared in the February 2017 e-newsletter of the Beverly Historical Society.

Colorful Characters Delivered the Mail
By Stephen P. Hall

No one today remembers seeing the main U.S. Post Office in Beverly other than at the corner of Rantoul and Broadway. But when this building was dedicated in 1911 it was, in fact the tenth location of a main post office building in town.

On December 26, 1636 it was decreed that John Stone's ferry would carry the mail to Beverly. Prior to that time, the people of Beverly had to go by ferry to Salem for their letters. The first post office building was established in Beverly in 1792 and was located on the corner of Cabot and Front Streets, in Dixie Tavern. Owner Asa Leach received his commission as postmaster from President Washington. The story goes that Asa would meet the ferry, place the mail for Beverly inside his top hat and walk back to the tavern/post office, where folks would drop by to get their mail.

For many years the mail was transported from Salem to Beverly by Woodbury Page in his stage coach the *Rambler*, until the Eastern Railroad extension was completed in 1842. Over the years the post office was moved often. Its seventh home was on the corner of Cabot Street and Railroad Avenue. It was a small store front with mail hanging on strings in the window. People would come by daily to look in the front window to see if they had any mail. It wasn't until 1886 that free home delivery was established.

At that time the post office was located in the Odd Fellows Block, on the Broadway side – its ninth location. That year, under the leadership of Francis Norwood four letter carriers were appointed, Josiah Woodbury, Martin Murry, William Hanners and John Foley. By 1908 the city had grown to 18,000 residents requiring 22 mailmen.

Main Post Office on Rantoul Street in the 1920s.

In 1901 one of the most colorful characters in the history of Beverly mail service was a crusty old "Marbleheader" named Captain Thomas Jefferson Peach. Tom Peach was born in 1839 and he learned the codfish business from his father, sailing for the Grand Banks for the first time when he was 16. After more than 20 years as a fisherman, Peach joined the army and fought in the Civil War. Various jobs followed his service including grocer and machinist and "ship's keeper" at the Charlestown Navy Yard. By 1900 he and his wife Ellen were living in Beverly, and at age 61 Tom Peach became a mailman.

Each day the train would bring the mail to Beverly Depot and Captain Peach with the assistance of his horse "Bob" and a small wagon would pack it up and deliver it to the Broadway Post Office. In the first years a single delivery was sufficient, but by 1911 he was making as many as three trips for a single mail. Captain Peach and Bob moved the mail seven days a week between the train station and the Post Office. In an interview in 1927, Peach said that in 1901 there were 12 mails a day and more than 20 in 1911. When the current building opened the railroad began delivering right to the Post Office. Peach remarked "The next day I sold my horse, wagon, and harness." As for Bob the horse, he went on delivering for a few more years, but this time for Mitchell's laundry.

A version of this article was published in the Winter 2006 issue of the *Chronicle*.

Chapter 4: Having Fun

Beverly's Lost Ballpark
By Edward R. Brown

Today, it is a residential neighborhood of five parallel streets connecting Essex Street to Odell Avenue--Hawthorne, Magnolia, Lowell, Sherman, and Bertram Streets. In the first decade of the 20th century, however, it was a park that echoed with the sound of baseballs cracking against wooden bats and the shouts of cheering spectators. It was called Peabody's Field, Beverly's primary baseball park.

The site of the ballpark was the property of the Prospect Hill Realty Trust, whose trustee and principal owner was Henry W. Peabody. Mr. Peabody was a wealthy businessman who, in his own name or through the real estate trusts he controlled, owned vast tracts of land in Beverly in the early 20th century. Some of those eventually became the housing developments on Prospect Hill and on the south side of Essex Street in the Montserrat neighborhood.

Peabody had a soft spot in his heart for Beverly and decided that the 13-acre stretch of land between Essex and Odell should be used for

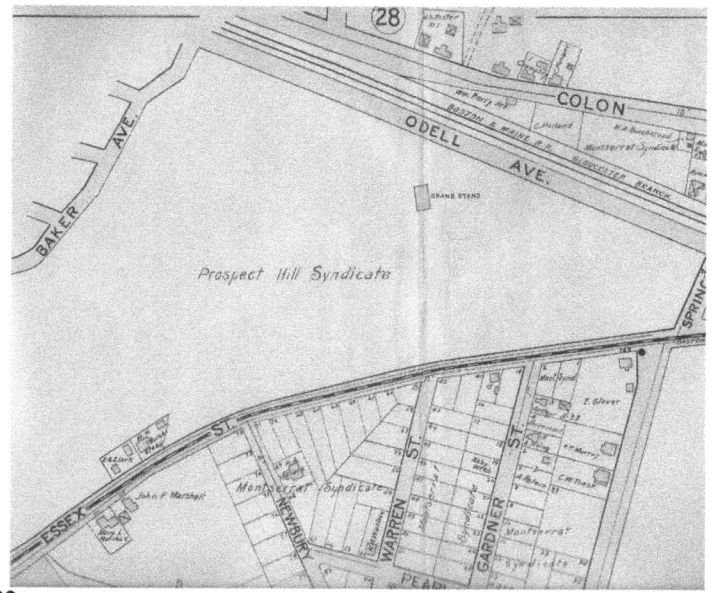

recreational purposes instead of house lots. He allowed the city to establish a baseball park on the site, complete with a grandstand and a fence to control access. Since streetcars ran right by the field on Essex Street, spectator access was easy, and the Montserrat train depot was also nearby for the convenience of visiting fans.

Beverly's high school team played its home games there. But the real attraction for baseball fans was the semi-pro ball club, managed by T. Richard "Dick" Madden. Madden's team featured the best ballplayers he could attract. The local team did not belong to any league but took on all comers from the baseball-mad towns in the area. In 1907 the Beverly club accepted a challenge from the Wakefield team to play a best-of-seven series for what was billed as the "championship of the state." So high was the excitement that Madden even chartered a special train to take Beverly fans to the "away" games. A series with Salem, to be played for a $100 prize, drew as many as 1,000 spectators. On the Fourth of July in 1907, Madden booked a home game against the Cuban Giants, a famous barnstorming team of the time, made up of African-American ballplayers who were barred from playing professional baseball. For big games, Madden didn't hesitate to bring in "ringers" from out of town to beef up the lineup, but hometown fans didn't seem to mind.

Madden also served as a scout for Connie Mack's major league Philadelphia Athletics. When Gloucester teenager John "Stuffy" McInnis joined the Beverly team as a 16-year-old in 1907, Madden knew he had a future star on his hands. Although he was less than 5'8" inches tall, Stuffy soon captured the hearts of Beverly fans with spectacular plays in his two seasons at Peabody's Field. In July of 1908, Connie Mack, at Madden's urging, signed both McInnis and Beverly pitcher Harold "Doc" Martin to major league contracts. Martin pitched only 14 games in the majors, but Stuffy went on to a stellar 18-year big league career, including six seasons in Boston.

Meanwhile, controversy was swirling around Peabody's Field. Mr. Peabody had offered to sell the entire 13-acre parcel to the city for $26,000 so that it could be kept as a sports facility. The Beverly Park Commissioners recommended that Beverly buy the field.

Commissioner Edmund Putnam, speaking in favor, said: "The price is low, location is good, taxpayers and summer residents favor it." Beverly High School students produced a resolution backing the purchase and a planning committee produced a blueprint that included the existing ballpark, a boy's baseball field, football field, track, croquet lawn and a shaded pavilion. It would be a community showplace.

But the city council dithered over the purchase throughout 1908. The editor of the *Beverly Evening Times* supported the purchase, so naturally the editor of the *Beverly Citizen* opposed it. Mayor S. Harvey Dow, a proponent of economizing, didn't seem enthusiastic. Then it was too late. Henry W. Peabody died on December 7, 1908. Although his obituary declared that "it was his desire that this plot should be taken by the city," the trustee of the real estate trust did not agree. Within weeks of Mr. Peabody's death surveyors were laying out five streets through the ballpark. In 1909 houses lots were advertised for sale – "Lots are large, prices small, $200 to $550, $25 down $5 monthly, no interest, no taxes." Beverly would be without a baseball field until Cooney Field was readied for play in 1912. But the vision of a community showplace that Peabody's Field had briefly promised was gone.

A version of this article appeared in the Spring 2017 issue of the *Chronicle*

When Little League Came to Town
by Edward R. Brown

Little League Baseball originated at Williamsport, Pennsylvania in 1939, when a man named Carl Stotz and a few friends started an organized program for boys 12 and under, on a field built to their size. They kept the idea alive through World War II, and with publicity after the war, it began to spread, especially after a national magazine published an illustrated article. Once growth began, Stotz incorporated the name and trademark, and accepted an offer from the U.S. Rubber Co. (now Uniroyal) to underwrite an office headquarters in

Williamsport. By 1949, several Connecticut communities had brought the program to New England.

Beverly was the first place in Massachusetts to adopt Little League, followed closely by Pittsfield. Its generation here can be traced to what was then Beverly's largest employer, the United Shoe Machinery Corporation (USMC). In the summer of 1949, several men made the drive to Stamford, Connecticut, which had a USMC branch and was one of the first Connecticut towns to start a league. The idea was talked up at the Beverly USMC plant. Several informal meetings were held in the fall of 1949, and it was agreed that Little League might work in Beverly.

In February of 1950, a meeting was held at the Beverly Chamber of Commerce. U.S. Rubber had assigned a team to travel and show "Little League movies" where interest was expressed. They came to Beverly the night of February 16, where about 20 men were on hand. They decided to organize a four-team league for that spring and summer and to apply for a charter. Joseph P. Nixon, president of Cor-Nix Rubber Company (Beverly's sporting goods store) and treasurer of the Chamber of Commerce, was elected the first president. Other officers chosen were Abbott Morse, vice president; Vin Hayes, secretary; Tom Tierney, treasurer; Larry Hayes, player agent; and John Carbone, umpire-in-chief. Managers of the four original teams, named for major league clubs, would be Dan Murphy for the Yankees, Ed Stokes for the Dodgers, Lou Appolloni for the Red Sox, and Frank Stackpole for the Braves (a team then still playing in Boston).

The new league wanted a field it would not have to share with another organization and where a Little League-sized diamond could be built. Mayor Robert J. Rafferty and public works commissioner Louis Harrigan offered an idea—Bessie Baker Park. That isolated tract of land between Cabot Street and Odell Avenue had been purchased with money left to the city by Bessie A. Baker, the civic-minded citizen who especially wanted park space for children and mothers. Nixon and Appolloni used a tape measure to inspect the place and determined there was just enough room for a Little League field. In March, the Board of Aldermen approved the proposed use, with a provision that

Baker's heirs had no objection (which led to a restriction that the park would be used by children no older than 12) and appropriated $500 to build a ball field.

The *Beverly Evening Times* printed an application form, and to everyone's surprise, 250 boys signed up. Tryouts were held that spring at Cooney Field. At a "player auction" conducted by Larry Hayes, each team manager chose 12 uniformed players plus three extras, who could be used only if a regular player was absent. Early box scores reveal that many times managers used only their starting nine players. To ease the disappointment for those not selected, a six-team "farm league" was organized, with two teams each based in Ryal Side, North Beverly, and downtown. On the afternoon of Sunday, June 11, 1950, Little League in Massachusetts was launched with two games at Bessie Baker Park. A snow fence surrounded the field that first season, replaced the next year by a permanent fence with a tall barrier, nicknamed "the monster" by the kids, to protect the homes on Odell Avenue from damage. Games were written up in the local paper and several hundred spectators attended the games. In August, an "all-star" team was chosen to represent Beverly against Pittsfield for the state championship and a chance to compete for the New England title and a possible trip to Williamsport for the Little League World Series. The Beverly contingent came home disappointed, claiming to have been robbed of a victory by a "home town decision."

With the interest shown throughout that first summer at Bessie Baker Park, a number of communities, including Danvers, Peabody, Salem, and Lynn started Little Leagues in 1951. Beverly was chosen to host the first full "final four" state tournament, which resulted in a massive volunteer effort. The host community was disappointed not to be involved, having been upset by Danvers, in what was then a single elimination tourney. A consolation prize was that the team was invited to play an exhibition game at Braves Field in Boston before a major league contest.

That '51 season started in spectacular fashion but ended in tragedy. The opening day game on May 20 featured a stellar pitching performance by two popular 11-year-olds, Vin Mallia of the Red Sox and Ed "Lefty" Josephs of the Braves, which brought headlines in the *Times* the next day. After the regulation six innings, both pitchers had not allowed a hit, sending the game to extra frames. Pitching rules at the time allowed both pitchers to continue for up to nine innings. The Sox finally scored the winning run in the seventh inning when Jackie DiRubio's base hit sent home Richie Tonneson, who had reached a base on balls. Mallia was on top of his game, but his friends and coaches began to notice a change as the season went along. It came to a head in an August playoff game when Appolloni recalled that he was forced to remove his faltering star from the game for his own safety. Doctors diagnosed a rare form of brain cancer, which took the popular youngster's life the

In 1952, the original four-team Beverly Little League expanded to six "major" teams, and to keep things in balance that year, all teams were re-drafted. Here is the 1952 Beverly Little League "all-star" team. Front row, left to right: Dave Richardson, John Maglio, Richie Tonneson, Danny Murphy, Billy Gasperoni, Gordon Reid. Back row: Manager Dan Murphy, Bob Walsh, Ted Doucette, Ed "Lefty" Josephs, Dick DePiero, Joe Balboni, Coach John DiRubio.

following January. A memorial in his honor was dedicated at the park that May.

Little League here quickly grew as more and more children turned out and the privately-funded program expanded to accommodate them. Its success opened the door for other sports organizations to launch their own programs. The original league was divided into two in 1955 and then three by 1960. Minor and farm divisions provided space for everyone, and for some years Beverly Little League was invited to become a United Way agency. From 1961 through the 1970s, it operated a "senior division" for ages 13 to 15 before turning that program over to the Beverly Babe Ruth League. By the 1980s, league officials were looking to build a home park that could have field lights and be a youth baseball showplace. The city agreed in 1993 to lease the little-used Centerville playground for the league to build upon. With the help of local contractors and merchants as well as its own fundraising efforts, the newly rechristened "Harry Ball" field blossomed into a facility with two lighted ball fields, roofed dugouts, clubhouse with refreshment stand and restrooms, permanent bleachers, paved off-street parking, and lighted scoreboards. Nicknamed Beverly's "field of dreams," it has hosted state tournaments and other events including the schools' "Momball" tournament.

The 21st century has seen a steady decline in enrollment, with Beverly Little League now back to its original status as a single league. But for those who love baseball, it is still as relevant as it was when the founders brought it to Beverly back in 1950.

A version of this article appeared in the 2017 e-newsletter of Historic Beverly.

Beverly's Famous Theatre
By Gail Balentine

During the 1890s and early 1900s, 286-290 Cabot Street was the site of a boarding house. In 1920, after the 'Great War' and on the cusp of the 'Roaring Twenties,' two brothers from Marblehead trans-formed the property and the downtown Beverly landscape. At what was then a

staggering cost of $250,000, D. Glover Ware and N. Harris Ware built the *Ware Theatre*. Funk and Wilcox were the architects of the neo-classical building, described by show-business magazine *Variety* as "the most impressive auditorium of its size east of New York." The building was indeed impressive with its elaborate marquee above the entrance and central ticket booth and its lobby faced with pink marble. The dome of its auditorium soared 43 feet over walls that were ornate with gold-leaf highlights and chandeliers that sparkled. Music was provided by a $50,000 Austin pipe organ. Although the organ is long gone, much of the original decoration in the auditorium has survived.

On Thursday evening, December 9, 1920, the *Ware Theatre* opened to much fanfare with the silent movie *Behold My Wife!* The advertisement for the grand opening included this statement: "Dedicated to the Playgoers of Beverly and Vicinity as a Shrine for the Proper Presentation of Silent Drama." For the initial performance, all seats were reserved at a cost of $0.55 per seat.

In 1920s there were about 20,000 such movie palaces throughout the country; only about 250 have survived. To be among those 250, residents and owners had to value the theatre and its rich history, and for the Ware Theatre that has been true. In 1960 the business was sold to E.M. Loew and renamed the Cabot Cinema. And from 1976 to 2013 it was the home of the renowned La Grand David magic show, drawing thousands of people from all over to see the live performances. When the magic company closed, the building's future was very much in doubt.

In this era of iPhones, iPads, cable television and Youtube, it may be tempting to underestimate the impact that such a place can have on a community. To find out, however, all you need do is ask residents how different downtown Beverly felt when the theatre was closed and its marquee dark. What a relief it was when in 2014 a group of civic-minded people rescued the nearly 100-year-old theatre, once again breathing life into both the venerable structure and the city of Beverly.

A version of this article appeared in the December 2017 e-newsletter of Historic Beverly.

Making Magic
By Edward R. Brown

From the time it was formed in 1977 and for the next three decades, "Le Grand David and His Own Spectacular Magic Company" attracted national publicity, rave reviews, and hordes of visitors to the company's two-hour Sunday afternoon productions in Beverly. It was the brainchild and dream of Cesario Pelaez, who grew up in Havana surrounded by great entertainment and the traveling magic shows of old. Cesario was forced to flee Cuba when Castro's Communist revolution came to power. He became a popular professor of psychology at Salem State College. But it was his great passion as an entertainer and magician which inspired a new venture in neighboring Beverly. In the late 1970s Pelaez recruited a number of friends who, as White Horse Productions, pooled their resources to buy the Cabot Theater, restoring it for live performances. David Bull joined the company in the demanding leading role of "Le Grand David." After much rehearsing the volunteer company was off and running, adding singing, dancing and juggling to the spectacular magical illusions. Cesario performed many of them himself as "Marco the Magi." Props were built and costumes sewn in the work rooms above the theater. Wanting a child lead performer, he picked young Seth Bartlett, whom he had known from infancy and who as "Seth the Sensational" wowed audiences for years. When Seth outgrew the role, the daughters of other cast members succeeded him. The reputation of the magic show grew and the cast was invited to Washington to perform at the White House many times. The company also bought the run-down Larcom Theater

Wall art on the Cabot Cinema features the cast of the famed magic show Le Grand David, c. 1997.

on Wallis Street which they cleaned up and modified for an occasional second version of the show.

Sadly, Cesario Pelaez became ill in 2007 and could no longer perform. The company which had once numbered 70 had dwindled to about 15 members; advance show tickets no longer were sold. It was clear that the end of an era was at nearly at hand. In tribute to their founder they kept going until they were able to celebrate a 30th anniversary show. Although the spectacular performances are over, the joy they brought to thousands linger in memory.

A version of this article appeared in the February 2015 e-newsletter of the Beverly Historical Society.

Chapter 6: Making a Living

Of Cod and Colonials

By John Cuffe

In the words of Harvard lecturer and renowned historian, Samuel Eliot Morison, "Stark necessity made seamen of would-be planters" And what fish did those colonial farmers turned mariners most prize? Cod.

Fish flake yards were found all along the Beverly coast and the Bass River.

In the 1770s, dried and salted Atlantic cod accounted for 35% of all exports from New England. The economic significance of this single fish stock swelled further when related maritime industries such as sail and rope making and ship building are considered. In the earliest days of the Massachusetts Bay Colony small towns dotted the coast. Their economies were largely agrarian, augmented by fish caught inshore by small shallops with two or three-man crews. By the mid-18th century, Massachusetts men were putting to sea in 35' to 65' full-decked vessels – the two-masted schooners which became the workhorse of the fishing fleets.

The crews of seven to eight men still sought cod, but they braved the vast Atlantic to locate their quarry. The "first fare" set out in the spring, with a second voyage in the fall. A week's sailing was often required to reach Sable Island, a prime fishing ground, 200 miles southeast of Nova Scotia. The skipper might anchor the schooner for three to four weeks. In that time each crewman might catch, on average, 1,500 fish; roughly 70 per man, per day. Accounts of the period reveal that Atlantic cod weighed between 5 and 100 pounds, with rare specimens reaching a staggering 200 pounds. Most fish were about 35 pounds each.

The waters of Sable Island Bank were 40 to 50 fathoms deep, which meant that a fisherman was perched 240 to 300 feet above his bottom-feeding prey. Once hooked, the sailor had to retrieve his catch with a hand-line. The effort was equivalent to hauling the fish up a 25-story building. Once the catch was aboard the fisherman only had to repeat the process another 69 times that day! At day's end he would sleep in the hold beside the wet-cured results of his, and his mates' labors, only to begin anew at dawn. It's small wonder that these hardy men were no longer fit for a life at sea by about age thirty. One astounding voyage under Captain Gideon Rea in the mid-18th century tallied 122,222 fish in a five-month voyage. That amounts to more than 100 fish a day for each man!

If luck held, their hold was filled when they returned home with the salted cargo, where the curing process was completed by drying on "fish flakes" – open racks where the fish were dried in the sun. Robert Rantoul noted that on a Sunday if it threatened rain, the men and boys dashed from church to cover the valuable catch. Sometimes called the "sacred cod" for its immense importance to the economy, many New England fortunes were made sending the fish to Catholic Europe for their meat-free Fridays with the broken bits and pieces traded to the West Indies to feed the slaves laboring on the sugar plantations. Dried cod was a staple here at home as well. As late as 1860, fifty-four vessels sailed from Beverly to the Atlantic fishing banks. The fleet carried 472 men, out of approximately 2000 males in town. The Civil War and the rise of shoe-making factories slowly brought an end to the industry that had sustained Beverly and other coastal towns for generations.

A version of this article appeared in the March 2017 e-newsletter of the Beverly Historical Society.

To Sumatra for Pepper 1806-1847
By Terri McFadden

In the wake of the American Revolution local merchants, long restricted by the British, began looking to open up new markets across the world. Beverly vessels joined the flood to find trading partners in ports as far-flung as Europe, India, China and southeast Asia. Among the most lucrative was the voyage to Sumatra in the East Indies seeking black pepper.

The pepper trade had been dominated for 200 years by Europeans, first by Portugal and later the Netherlands. It wasn't until 1785 when a Salem vessel, the *Grand Turk* owned by Elias Hasket Derby, sailed to Sumatra that Americans began to get into this valuable trade. That first voyage secured a 700% profit and even after many ships from Beverly and Salem got involved in the trade, a successful trip could make hundreds of times the owner's investment.

Logs and business records of many voyages spanning more than forty years give a hint of the dangers and difficulties of maritime trade. The journey was a long one. A ship's crew could expect to be away from home for 18 months to two years, depending on sailing conditions, the number of ports they called on and the time it took to load cargo. Pirates and reefs were ever-present dangers along the Sumatra coast and both disease and accidents at sea made sea-faring a very dangerous business.

The Beverly ship *Alexander Hodgdon* left Beverly harbor on Saturday, September 20, 1806 bound for Sumatra under the command of Josiah Lovett. Just three days into the voyage an English frigate stopped the American ship and sent an officer on board to examine her papers. Things were apparently in order and they were "permitted to proceed." On the eighth day out, the log records "a large sea at 1pm [sent] the ship Rolling Very bad, rolled away the fore and main top masts over the side…." The ship had also sustained serious damage to the rigging and several sails were torn away. Two men were swept overboard but fortunately were rescued.

Over the next eight days Captain Lovett had "all hands employed" raising masts, re-rigging, and repairing the damage. A painting of the vessel shows the extent of the damage and captures the crew as they scramble to repair the ship. When restored, the *Alexander Hodgdon* resumed its voyage; the lure of pepper a siren song for 19th century mariners and merchants alike.

A version of this article appeared in Beverly Historical Society's Spring 2012 *Chronicle*.

"Everything very Scarce here but Musketoes": The trials of the Vancouver

By Terri McFadden

For many years the city of Archangel was a major Russian port. When St. Petersburg was built in the early 18th century the Czar decreed that no maritime commerce was to go through the older port. The ban lasted until 1762, when the vast resources in the region again became a draw for merchant vessels. There was however, a very short window to trade. The port was iced in for five months of the year.

Captain Michael Whitney and his Beverly crew sailed out of Boston on April 7, 1812 bound for Archangel, hoping to be home with a full hold in less than a year. First mate Andrew Standley kept the log of the brig, the *Vancouver*. They made good time to the port on the White Sea, taking just two months to make the voyage. During their time at anchor, Standley recorded the cargo the crew loaded, among them wood, iron, beef, glass, and "bale goods" – animal skins. On August 10th they proceeded down the river, were piloted across the Archangel Bar and out to sea.

Ten days into the voyage home Standley recorded the bad news: "…at ½ past 3pm spoke with the Schooner *Conholm*…informed us of a Declaration of War with England – Captain thought Proper to make the first Port of Safety…." Back they sailed to Archangel.

Mr. Standley recorded the activities of the crew for the next weeks as they waited, hoping for news that they could sail for home. They were "employed in knotting yarns and spinning them," doing "sundry" shipboard tasks, and "making sennet" (braiding rope). The first heavy snowfall occurred on the 20th of September. Realizing they were trapped in Archangel, Captain Whitney employed all hands in preparing the *Vancouver* for the long, dark Russian winter. They removed the cargo so recently stowed and cleared the decks of lumber. Soon the men had to cut ice from the hull and cables. On November 11th they left the ship for a nearby village, leaving just one man on board. First Mate Standley and others visited the brig periodically to check her for soundness and crews were employed regularly to keep the hull free of crushing ice.

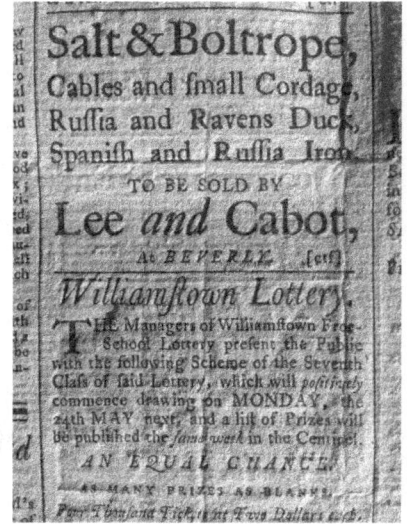

Lee and Cabot Advertisement for salt & cordage, which all ships needed. Boltrope is the rope that is sewn at the edges of the sail to reinforce them, or to fix the sail into a groove in the boom or in the mast.

On the 10th of May the signal came from the castle overlooking the town that the ice was broken; the first sign of spring. Summer in Archangel region proved, if anything, to be worse than the long bitterly cold winter. In mid-June the first "musketoes" made their appearance. Nearly every day Mr. Standley recorded the misery suffered by the men. His other regular comment was "Nothing worth remarking," underscoring their boredom. They hoped for news that the war was over, but all summer vessels arrived with "no news." Finally, in August of 1813 news of home arrived, but it was bad. The Americans learned of the loss of the *Chesapeake* to the British frigate *Shannon*. The *Vancouver* and her crew spent two more years in Russia, suffering from cold, insufficient food and the summer scourge of "musketoes." At long last they weighed anchor on June 26, 1815 bound for the United States. First Mate Standley wrote fervently "God send us a Safe and Speedy passage." They were away from home and loved ones for more than three and half years.

A version of this article appeared in the Beverly Historical Society's Fall 2012 *Chronicle*.

My Loving Friend
By Terri McFadden

Mariner Nathaniel Allen's letters to his "loving friend" – his wife Anna – give a glimpse into the lives of an ordinary Beverly man in the early 19th century. The first letter was written before they married and twenty-year-old Nathaniel expresses understanding about Anna's concerns for him as he is about to leave on a voyage. He advises her: "It will not do to let your mind dwell too much on such things, for we must expect to meet with such disappoint[ment] in this world…." In January 1812 the couple were married.

A little over a year later Anna received a letter written from a prison ship anchored in Chatham, England. It is evident from the text that Anna hadn't heard from her husband since he was captured by the British in August of 1812. Nathaniel's experience didn't keep him from his trade as a mariner. In the years following his release, letters from Bordeaux, France describe the "agreeable voyage, a good ship and an agreeable crew." The next few years saw him sailing on fishing vessels. Always he expresses his wish to be with her and their "dear children." By 1820 they had four. A memorable voyage to the fishing banks in 1821 found him writing about his fellow crew members which he described as "…the most Abandoned Characters in Drunkenness & Blasphemy, Sabbath Breaking, and all manner of Vice & wickedness.

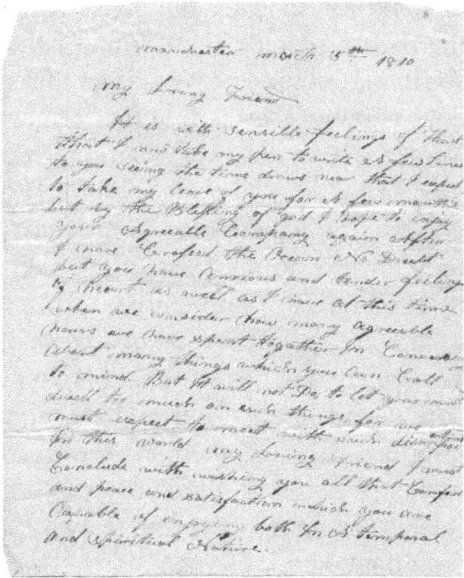

Letter from Nathanial Allen to his wife Anna.

Clearly Nathaniel was a thinking man as well as a religious one. In 1821 he wrote Anna, asking if she "Sees more and more of the vanity of Earthy [sic] Objects…and the folly of placing your Affections On Created Objects" rather than on Christ.

Nathaniel Allen died while on a voyage to Genoa, Italy in 1822 at age 32, leaving not only his wife and children, but these written hints of a life, both ordinary and profound.

A version of this article appeared in the November 2014 e-newsletter of the Beverly Historical Society.

Gold Fever, Beverly Style

By Terri McFadden

Like many Americans in 1849, Beverly men were stirred with a mixture of adventure and greed by the news of the gold strike in California. As word spread of the fortunes that could be made, mining and trading companies were formed; three here in Beverly alone. Other local men joined companies in Boston, Salem and other New England communities. Isaac W. Baker wrote: "Members of a society could be told by their slouched hats, high boots, careless attire and a general appearance of reckless daring and potential wealth."

Each company had written by-laws stipulating conduct and business expectations. The proprietors bought shares which helped to raise money for travel expenses, cargo and tools for the gold fields. Some men, unable to afford to purchase shares in the company, worked off their fees. There were several ways to get to California; overland, a sea route and a mixture of sea and land. As coastal town residents many of the prospective miners were mariners by trade. Beverly men overwhelmingly chose the sea routes – either sailing around Cape Horn or through the Gulf of Mexico and crossing to the Pacific Ocean.

Local businesses, hoping to attract miners preparing for the journey, advertised products including "Extract of Canchlagua to purify the blood – something every miner will need." The newspapers gave a curious mixture of encouragement and descriptions of dangers the miners would be facing. Reports of cholera and other diseases that killed hundreds were printed in a local paper. The same article stated that "California remains healthy." Miners were told to expect martial law and that claim-jumpers were lynched, but noted "it is safer than previously."

The dire warnings of danger didn't deter many. Men of all ages and walks of life dropped everything for the lure of gold. Getting to California was dangerous, no matter what route was chosen. The longest way in terms of miles was south around Cape Horn and north to San Francisco. Fierce storms could keep vessels from going "round the Horn" for months. But sometimes this way was the quickest choice.

One local ship, the *San Francisco*, left Beverly harbor in August of 1849. A diarist described the scene as the whole town turned out to see the ship depart, "leaving weeping women and cheering men and boys." The miners on board the *San Francisco* were "lucky dogs;" their voyage was one of the swiftest recorded at just 149 days. Some vessels sailed through the Gulf of Mexico and then the miners crossed Panama where they were forced to wait for weeks for another ship heading north. Texas and Mexico were other routes favored by the would-be miners. Each journey was dangerous in its own way. Local builder, Warren Prince, age 36, left his wife and three children hoping to strike it rich. Instead he and his company, while crossing Texas, ran out of food, were forced to drink polluted water and six came down with cholera. Five of them died. Prince survived but his gold hunting days were over.

The barque San Francisco *made the trip "round the horn" in record time.*

The owners of the *San Francisco* hoped to cash in on the building boom in the burgeoning town of San Francisco amid the scarcity of supplies. The plan was to sell the cargo before heading the 150 miles inland to the gold fields. The vessel carried boards, bricks, and frames for houses, worth the princely sum of $25,000 (more than $630,000 today).

Problems arose as soon as the ship arrived in California. Just a few men stayed with the ship in order to unload and sell her cargo, the rest abandoned the company in a dash to find gold. In the months since they had sailed from Beverly the price of building supplies had plummeted by nearly 70% and they were forced to sell at a loss. Master of the *San Francisco*, Thomas Remmonds described the filthy boom town where dead horses were left to rot in the muddy streets and there was "nothing going on here but gambling and drinking…prices of almost all things are very high." Boots that sold for $2.50 in Beverly went for $25.00 in California.

Word came back home of the fate of some of the men; wives and sweethearts recorded the bad news in their diaries. Sarah Trask wrote that of nine couples who were close friends all the men had joined the ranks of miners and all but four of them had died. Her fiancée, Luther Woodbury perished on the voyage around Cape Horn. "I have seen my Best friend on earth, Depart for a far Country, with bright prospects before him and my hope was, that he would do well, and return safely…how vain were my hopes, for Death has claimed him for his own."

There is no record that any Beverly men made a fortune in the gold fields of California. Yet the lure of gold fever survived long after the boom. One young man, a child when his older brother had gone west, left home without a word nearly ten years after the first news of California gold. His family heard nothing from him for two years, until broke and ill he managed to return home – the promise of riches still unfulfilled.

A version of this article appeared in the Beverly Historical Society's Summer 2011 issue of the *Chronicle*.

Agriculture in a Coastal Town
By Meike Gourley

Beverly's glorious maritime history of privateering, fishing and long-distance trade is well-known and justly celebrated. The painting by local artist Avis Thomas *Beverly in 1700* shows the docks, cod drying racks, and sailing vessels. But if you look just a little inland you will see crops and meadows, orchards and a variety of domestic animals. Although New England soil is notoriously rocky, farmers made their living with it from the earliest days until well into the 20th century.

Fields around Beverly about 1840. Detail from A. Thomas painting

Beverly was a lively agricultural town, with about half its residents making their living from the soil in the 1670s. They grew hay, corn, rye, barley, apples, potatoes and beans. For clothing the settlers used wool sheared from their sheep and grew flax to produce linen. In the earliest days of settlement domestic animals were too valuable to be killed for food. The land around the town was filled with deer and other wild game that were hunted and eaten. Later, when the number of domestic animals increased, farmers could afford to kill more of their animals for food. It was the custom to share the meat of the animal with the neighbors and to get repaid later when it was their turn to slaughter one of their animals. Meat not immediately consumed was salted and it "kept for a number of months before all was eaten." Farmers kept their preserved beef and pork in barrels called "powdering tubs." Cattle, pigs, horses, dogs, donkeys and poultry all were part of farm life. Town records give an idea of how animal husbandry changed over the centuries. In 1767 the count was 1099 sheep and just 37 swine. In 1840 there were more than 900 swine, whereas the number of sheep had dropped to only 180.

In order to protect the fields and common land from damage by stray animals, the town had very strict laws on setting up and maintaining fences, walls and hedges. The town selectmen had the duty to choose an overseer of fences. All the fences that came under his supervision had to be repaired between March 30th and April 12th. Landowners were required to maintain their own fences around cultivated land and to help with setting up fences around common land.

Strict rules served to protect crops from animals roaming freely; a fine was charged to anyone breaking the rules. In Wenham cattle were forbidden to roam into the "common field wherein corne is growing until the corne be gathered out of ye field upon the penalty of two shilling six pence per head." Pigs were allowed to run free during the fall and winter, but during the growing season they had to be controlled to prevent them from destroying crops. Beverly town records state that "all swine above three month old shall be ringed & yoaked."

Sheep and rams were strictly separated to control breeding. At a town meeting in 1705 it was voted that rams were not allowed to be with ewes on the Town Common between August 15th and the end of October. Horses too caused some concern. In 1691 "field drivers" were chosen to capture "stone horses" (stallions) and colts that were roaming freely in the commons and woods. No stallion above the age of two was to be allowed in the common lands, "unless he be of comely proportion & sufficient stature, not less than fourteen hands high…."

Although the importance of agriculture in the local economy is long in the past, it's interesting to learn how well-organized and carefully managed the land was. Selectmen, fence overseers, field drivers, pond keepers and others helped the local farmers produce the necessities crucial to sustain the life of the community.

A version of this article appeared in the Fall 2017 issue of the *Chronicle*.

Friend's Mill
By Darren Brown and Terri McFadden

Friend's Mill, a tidal mill, was in operation for 238 years, late 19th c. photograph

Few firms can claim to have stayed in business more than two centuries, but the tidal gristmill that stood at the head of the Bass River was in active operation for 238 years. The remains of the mill can still be seen at low tide next to Elliott Street at the foot of McKay Street and one of the stone grinding stones is on display outside the Cummings Center; both are evidence of early industry in Beverly. Mills were an important part of early colonial communities, providing products like sawn lumber and flour for residents. We know that there were several mills in town from an early date, but Friend's Mill was one of the first.

In 1647 John Friend secured waterpower rights and he soon dammed the river to obtain power for his mill. Although Friend was the builder and original owner he wasn't in the picture for long. A few years later Lawrence Leach put 10 pounds down and promised to pay another 30 pounds to purchase the business. He never managed to repay the debt, but eventually his son, John Leach, purchased the thriving business and ran it until 1670.

The next owner was John Dodge, Jr. and he and his descendants operated the mill until 1797. Thomas Davis, Jr. purchased the mill in 1797 for $2850, including "two grist mills…with mill dam, flumes, timber, also all the mill privilege of the stream waters…." The word "mills" did not necessarily mean separate structures but referred to multiple sets of millstones.

Stephens Baker was born in 1791. His family owned a farm on what is today Beckford Street. He later remembered his childhood chore of riding a horse to the gristmill with grain to be ground for the weekly baking.

The last owner to use the mill to grind grain was Israel Dodge beginning in 1871. For a short time, the old mill on Elliott Street was used to grind old rubber. On June 4, 1885 a fire broke out, destroying most of the structure, a sad but spectacular end to one of Beverly's longest running businesses.

A version of this article appeared in the May 2014 e-newsletter of the Beverly Historical Society.

Beverly's Cotton Mill
By Edward R. Brown

"At the factory, a number of females were arranged, holding pieces of cloth in their laps for inspection. The General passed through the building, examining the machinery which was in operation. He stopped opposite Miss Francis...and examined the cloth in her lap. On leaving the factory he entered a carriage (his servant riding his horse) and proceeded to Ipswich."
Isaac Babson, eyewitness to President Washington's visit to the Beverly Cotton Mill in October 1789.

President Washington, after a personal inspection of the new cotton mill at Beverly, reported they were producing goods "excellent of their kind." That mill, which opened for production in January of 1789, was the first such operation in the new United States. Claims have been made that the Slater Mill in Pawtucket, Rhode Island was the first, but historian Robert S. Rantoul established that Mr. Slater did not arrive in America until January of 1790, and that his mill did not begin operations until the following year. Slater's partner acknowledged that Beverly's operation was the "first and largest."

An artist's idea of President Washington's Visit on October 30, 1787. Baker's Tavern is to the left and the three-story cotton mill to the right. Today this is the site of the North Beverly Fire Station.

The prime movers for the Beverly Cotton Mill were wealthy merchant John Cabot along with his business agent, Dr. Joshua Fisher. Incorporation papers drawn up in June of 1788 included the names of John, Andrew and George Cabot; their sister Deborah Cabot and other leading local figures, including Israel Thorndike and Nathan Dane. In August of 1788 Josiah and Hannah Batchelder sold to John Cabot and Joshua Fisher about five acres near Baker's Corner (now the site of the North Beverly Fire Station) to serve as the location for the new cotton factory. Two recent arrivals from Britain, Thomas Somers and James Leonard built the machinery to be used in the mill, Britain having banned the export of such machinery to their former colonies.

To house the mill, they erected a 60 by 25-foot three story brick building with a deep basement. When the mill opened for business in January 1789, 40 workers were employed and apprentices were enrolled by June. The largest of the machines was a spinning jenny capable of spinning 60 threads at a time. This fed a long row of looms where workers made corduroy, denim and other types of cloth. To provide power, a large spindle was seated in the basement. Two heavy draft horses turned the spindle, and 14-year-old Peter Homans was employed for the tedious task of leading those horses around and around all day.

Although the Slater Mill in Pawtucket followed the Beverly mill into operation, it had a major advantage. It was powered by a water wheel, many times more efficient than Beverly's horse-powered spindle. As a result, the pioneer cotton-making factory was relatively short-lived. Subsequent proprietors attempted a water wheel operation at the head of the Bass River, which was soon abandoned as unprofitable. The original mill building was destroyed by fire in 1828. Today a simple plaque marks the site of this early experiment in American manufacturing.

A version of this article appeared in the December 2016 e-newsletter of the Beverly Historical Society.

The Essex Bridge
By Gail Balentine

On August 2, 1996, with great fanfare and an estimated crowd of 17,000 people in attendance, the current Beverly-Salem bridge was officially opened. On that day, many residents breathed a sigh of relief – an end to the long waits for boats with tall masts to pass through during the summer! However, what people may not have realized at that time was the rich history of the former bridge, the Essex Bridge. And, the whole process of constructing it began with a famous signature...

When Beverly was established as a township in 1668, the only direct route to Salem was by ferry across the Bass River. Subject to weather, it was closed during much of the winter when ice clogged the harbor. As the population grew, such long lines occurred that taverns were built on both sides to accommodate those waiting for passage. The alternative to the ferry was a long ride through Danvers to Salem. Something needed to be done.

After the Charles River Bridge was constructed in 1786, Beverly residents were inspired to build one of their own and petitioned the General Court to do so. Salem mounted a vigorous opposition to the bridge, citing ferry toll losses and a concern that the bridge would block their fishing fleet. Danvers was also opposed, fearful of lost revenue due to less traffic through their town. However, on November 17, 1787

View of Cabot Street from the Beverly-Salem Bridge c. 1890. Photo by Lizzie Mitchell

the petition was signed by Governor John Hancock with the following specific provisions: the bridge would be a drawbridge through which vessels could pass day or night; tolls could be charged for "70 years and no more" to cover expenses and reimburse the investors; the bridge must be completed within four years or approval would be revoked; and, after 70 years the bridge would be turned over to the Commonwealth, free and clear. In an effort to address the opposition's concerns, the Court required that Beverly pay Salem 40 pounds per year and Danvers 10 pounds to make up for lost revenue during the 70 years that tolls would be collected.

Beverly investors got right to work on plans for building the bridge; financing the entire project privately. Construction costs totaled $16,000 (equivalent to more than $432,000 today). Two hundred shares were originally sold for $100 per share. By 1816 shares sold for $400 each. Over the 70 years investors realized an average dividend of 28%.

The bridge was begun in May of 1788 and completed four months later. At completion the bridge was 1,484 feet long, 32 feet wide, with 93 piers supporting it. At the time it was built, drawbridges were not common and there was much excitement about its operation. President George Washington came to Beverly to see it in operation on October 30, 1789. The original mechanism he viewed, which allowed for a lateral opening of the center of the bridge to accommodate vessels, was renovated in 1897 to open horizontally. On September 24, 1858, tolls were abolished and the Essex Bridge was turned over to the commonwealth.

A version of this article appeared in the September 2016 e-newsletter of the Beverly Historical Society.

The Old Corner Drugstore
By Terri McFadden

We are used to rapid changeover in the commercial world, businesses come and go. In the modern era it is unusual for a business to survive thirty years. However, this was not always the case. Robert Rantoul (1778-1858) started his apothecary shop here in Beverly in 1796. The door closed on the "Old Corner Drugstore" 144 years later. For all but its first two years this business stood at 151 Cabot Street on the corner of Washington Street.

A confident young man, Rantoul started his business when he was just 17, using a small inheritance, after serving an apprenticeship with a Salem druggist. For the first year he operated out of rented space, by his second year in business he was successful enough to build a small shop. By 1801 he had expanded into a two-story building of 24 by 40 feet, which was the home of the drugstore until its final closing. Rantoul imported herbs, medicines and other goods from the West Indies, and he had suppliers in London as well. In turn, he acted as a supplier to apothecaries and doctors in nearby towns and as far away as New Hampshire. The apothecary mixed his own medicines from herbs, alcohol and other ingredients and rolled his own pills. In addition to medicine, the shop also sold groceries and "dry goods," which included clothing, cloth and thread.

Mortar & pestle sign from the old corner drugstore.

By 1814 Rantoul had tired of the daily round of shop-keeping and turned his considerable talents to other endeavors. His former apprentice, Francis Lamson was entrusted with the business, while Rantoul retained ownership. Later his son-in-law, William Endicott and grandson Robert R. Endicott, took over the business. The mortar and pestle shop sign and the apothecary cabinet from the days of Rantoul and Endicott have survived in the collection of Historic Beverly.

Cabot Street, looking toward Salem in the second half of the 19th century when the pharmacy (left, front) was owned by Robert Rantoul Endicott, grandson of the founder

In the late 19th century and into the 20th, the drugstore changed hands about every 25 years. The last year of operation for the venerable shop was 1940. The building itself was torn down in the 1960s, making way for parking lot. A rather sad ending for a business patronized by generations of Beverly citizens.

A version of this article appeared in the February 2015 e-newsletter of the Beverly Historical Society.

A Different Spin

By Gail Balentine

Israel Trask was born on October 24, 1786 in Beverly. As was the custom of the times the young man was apprenticed, learning the trade of silversmith from local craftsman John Ellingwood. Trask later purchased the business from his master. Rather than silver, Trask began to produce more affordable pewter teapots, sugar bowls and other hollowware, but came to national prominence for his beautiful Britanniaware.

This alloy of tin, antimony and copper is similar to pewter, but the fabrication and sheen differ greatly from traditional cast pewter pieces. Britanniaware pieces were made by cold-forming the metal in sheet form by spinning or stamping, making possible a wider variety of shapes with thinner walls.

Legend has it that Israel Trask met a woman who complained that the British embargo of 1807 meant that no new teapots were available. He told her to gather her old spoons and pots and pans he would craft a new teapot.

The teapot he created was unusual, an oval shape with a wooden handle and it had engraved decorations, an embellishment previously reserved for silver pieces. Housewives appreciated the attractiveness of the everyday ware, which was harder, lighter and resisted tarnish. Trask had a true artisan's feel for the material and used designs and techniques that brought out the considerable beauty of the metal. His work can be found in major museums, including Metropolitan Museum in New York City. Historic Beverly is fortunate to have a fine collection of Trask's Britanniaware, as well as a selection of some of his tools. Trask continued to work in his Cabot Street until near the end of his long life. He died in 1867.

A version of this article was printed in the June 2015 e-newsletter of the Beverly Historical Society.

Bicycles Made Like a Watch
By Edward R. Brown

Chances are you've never heard of the "Raven" bicycle, made in Beverly, or its originator, William W. Marshall – known as W.W. But if you lived in town during the 1890s, you might have owned one.

Mr. Marshall was a man of many talents who had a decidedly up-and-down career. He first appears in the Beverly town directory in 1884; his occupation listed as a shoemaker, a common trade of the time. But he certainly had a broader vision and ambition. By 1893 he had a business of his own at 24 ½ Cabot Street, "…dealer in bicycles, tricycles, sundries, sporting goods and all the latest wheels." In the Gay Nineties, "wheels" was a term for any type of bicycle. By the next year,

W.W. Marshall began to manufacture by hand the two-wheeler he proudly named the "Raven."

By 1897 he was prosperous enough to take out a full-page in the Naumkeag Directory featuring his photo; that of a dapper mustachioed young man, and the words "Raven Bicycles" in large print, noting that the bicycles were built by him. He was proud of his work which in three years had "…not a broken frame or fork yet," and that the "wheels are made of the best material that can be got, and made like a watch…buy a Raven and be happy."

Mr. Marshall didn't content himself with just building bicycles. He was also a dealer in hardware, seeds, garden tools, wood ware, loaded shells, cutlery, paints and dog collars – to name just a few items advertised. Just about anything one wanted could be had by visiting his shop located at the lower intersection of Cabot and Rantoul near Cox Court.

The printed record of Marshall's business fades for six years. During that period, it is apparent that he experienced severe financial reverses. When the record picks up again in 1903, not only had he stopped selling bicycles, he was no longer in business. Instead, he was employed as a clerk on the premises of a former competitor, the Whitcomb Carter hardware store. Soon he moved on, finding a position as an inspector at the recently arrived United Shoe Machinery Corporation.

But visions of entrepreneurship and being his own boss must still have burned bright in the mind of W.W. Marshall. The growing popularity of the automobile led him on, and in 1908 he opened the North Shore Automobile Station at 146 Hale Street, in the heart of the Cove neighborhood. He made repairs to both foreign and American cars and for residents wishing to show off a really fancy ride, Marshall rented "touring cars by hour, day or week."

Sadly, for W.W., that operation was short-lived as well. By 1912 the station was out of business, sold to Pliny Hussey. Hussey's Garage became a Cove landmark for years to come. Marshall's bad luck in business continued when he opened and closed another garage in Danvers and he later made his living as a carpenter. For just a short while in the 1890s, W.W. Marshall was a big man in Beverly, with his fine Raven bicycle – made like a watch.

A version of this article appeared in the e-newsletter of the Beverly Historical Society.

A Chilly Business

By Darren Brown

At 13 years of age Boston-born Frederick Tudor (1783-1864) was so interested in pursuing a business career that he decided against going to Harvard, as his older brothers had. At 21, Tudor determined how he was going to make his fortune – providing wealthy Bostonians with ice. From Tudor's point of view, ice had two things going for it. It was both inexpensive and plentiful. It wasn't long before Tudor expanded his markets to the warm places in the world, where ice was viewed almost as a miracle in the days before refrigeration. The first few decades brought about both financial success and failure as Tudor experimented with ways to store and ship ice. Many of his cargos melted before they reached their destinations, leaving him deep in debt. He persevered, finding methods

Men pulling cut ice from Wenham Lake in the early 20th Century

to keep the ice frozen during the sea voyages and in insulated icehouses. Known as the "Ice King" Tudor held a monopoly in the industry for years.

As worldwide demand for ice grew, competitors were finally able to make their way into the market. The Wenham Lake Ice Company was created when Salem's Charles Lander began purchasing land in Wenham along the northeastern corner of Wenham Lake. Icehouses with an insulation barrier of hay, sawdust and wood shavings were constructed along the water's edge. A railway spur was added to connect the property to the main line and to seaports along the coast.

Workers are raising blocks to go up the conveyor to the ice house for storage.

Harvesting ice was much more complex than simply sawing chunks from a frozen pond. Following a snowfall, employees would "sink the pond" by systematically cutting small holes every few feet. This enabled water to spread evenly through the holes, transforming the snow into ice. After a few weeks of extremely low temperatures the ice reached an optimum thickness of 15 inches and would be ready for harvesting. The top layer was scraped by a horse-drawn scraper, removing all snow. Then a plow was used to create grooves in the ice. Blocks were sawn by hand along the furrows and the blocks pried out of the water. Men with poles pushed the blocks up to slides connected to the ice houses. Originally the slides were powered by horses and later steam was used to convey the ice into storage. When the ice was ready to ship, employees would load the blocks onto insulated railroad cars, each of which could hold five tons, about 250 blocks. The rail cars took the ice to Charlestown, where it was shipped to Europe.

About 30% of the cargo melted on the voyage, but this was far lower than the loss experienced by other companies, which was as much as 75%. The theory was that Wenham Lake ice was purer, preventing so much melt. True or not, the Beverly company's product became a necessity at all society events and is said to be the only type of ice used by Queen Victoria. Eventually, European sources began to undercut the Wenham Ice Company, especially those from Scandinavia, though the purity of our local ice still resonated in England. A lake in Norway was actually renamed "Lake Wenham" to continue the branding for the English market. For a few more decades ice continued to be shipped to foreign ports, until a massive fire destroyed most of the icehouses.

W.A. Caldwell Ice Company was one of a number of Beverly firms that cut and delivered ice locally.

Ice sales continued locally well into the 20th century. The Beverly Ice Company was founded in 1912 by John C. Kelleher. He located his delivery business at the corner of West Dane and Park Streets. For a time, he too harvested ice from Wenham Lake, but in the 1920s he purchased land on Essex Street to construct his own pond. The earth removed from Kelleher's Pond was transported to Central Cemetery to fill in the lowest section. Customers for Kelleher and other local ice dealers, F.B. Davis, Ernest Wright, W.A. Caldwell and B.N. Dodge, placed cards in their windows to notify drivers of the size of their order. Chunks of ice weighing between 15 to 30 pounds were carried into the kitchens of local homes and placed in the ice-box. Slowly the necessity for ice came to an end as people began buying electric refrigerators.

One senior citizen remembered that in the 1940s her mother didn't have the heart to tell Mr. Kelleher for two weeks that she no longer needed ice. Frederick Tudor's strange notion of selling ice transformed the way the world preserved food and for a hundred years Beverly citizens participated in this important industry.

A version of this article appeared in the Fall 2015 issue of the *Chronicle*.

Everything in the Food Line
By Edward R. Brown

It is long forgotten now, but a century ago downtown Beverly food shoppers were drawn to the pre-mises of Marston & Sturtevant, centrally located at 278 Cabot Street at the corner of Pond Street. Their advertisement in the 1911 City Directory claimed they were, "Grocers, bakers, provision and fish dealers." Special attention was given to fitting out yachts and parties. The modern convenience of the telephone made it easier for customers to place orders and, "teams cover all parts of the city. We supply all your wants." Later ads told buyers that Marston & Sturtevant sold "Everything in the Food Line."

Photographs show a thriving business with several counters and a large staff. The store was clean, well-lit and laid out in an orderly fashion. The business dated back to the 1890s and regular advertisements appeared in the City Directories just a few years later. In 1893 Marston & Sturtevant was located at 302 Cabot Street, but by 1897 the store was moved to what became its permanent home.

The founders retired in the 1920s, but two of Mr. Marston's children continued with the family business. The Great Depression, along with customers shopping at the new chain markets such as Stop & Shop and the A&P, seemed to be more than Marston & Sturtevant could overcome. By 1933, after more than 40 years in business, the store closed its doors forever.

A version of this article appeared in the November 2017 e-newsletter of Historic Beverly.

Nehemiah Heron Was a Busy, Busy Man
By Edward R. Brown

Doubt his story if you can, the Great-Grandfather was a busy, busy man.
Bo Diddley

Nehemiah S. Heron poses with the teachers at the Washington School where he was the custodian

In early 1900s Beverly, it is a wonder that Nehemiah S. Heron found time to do half of the jobs he was assigned to, much less enjoy any leisure moments. The 1906 city auditor's report reveals that he was paid $475 to serve as custodian of the Washington School, equal to about $10,000 today. That wasn't all of Mr. Heron's school responsibilities. He received another $360 in 1906 as Beverly's sole truant officer, tasked with chasing down both habitual truants, as well as those who "played hooky" occasionally. For that post, he had an office at 3 Broadway, in the Odd Fellows building.

He also found time to serve as sexton of the Washington Street Church, responsible for cleaning and polishing, moving furniture and ringing the bell. As an indication that Mr. Heron wasn't a hard-hearted truant officer but genuinely cared for children, he held another important position as Beverly's general agent for the Massachusetts Society for the Prevention of Cruelty to Children. Obviously, he found that youngsters had more than a pursuit of illicit pleasure as a reason for reluctance to attend classes. In his role as agent he helped with the serious problems that some children experienced.

Somehow the busy Mr. Heron also managed to maintain his own business on Charnock Street, where he and his wife, Henrietta resided. As early as 1897 and into the early 20th century Heron placed advertisements reading: "N.S. Heron -Furniture Repairer and Dealer in Rattan." He offered fix chairs that needed to be "re-caned, re-seated, stained and varnished. Re-seating lawn settees and chairs a specialty." Lest anyone think he did such work when he got around to it, he pledged: "All orders promptly attended to."

Mr. Heron kept up his multitasking ways until 1915. By that time, the truant officer position had expanded to such an extent that he began devoting all of his time and efforts to it. Eventually, he had his own office in the high school, where he kept office hours, before heading out to catch truants. All through the years of the First World War, Heron stuck to those duties, until he put aside his earthly cares with his death on January 26, 1919. After that, Beverly's truant students would have had to find someone else to chase after them.

A version of this article appeared Beverly Historical Society's Fall 2016 *Chronicle*.

Recalling Businesses Past: Ye Brunswick Music Shoppe
By Edward R. Brown

For more than 30 years, from the 1920s to the mid-50s, lovers of music would gather at 266 Cabot Street, in the heart of the thriving downtown Beverly shopping district, where the quaintly named Ye Brunswick Music Shoppe had its quarters.

The store had its beginnings in 1923, amid the Roaring 20s, when optimism prevailed and nobody dreamed that the good times wouldn't last forever. Ye Brunswick's founder and proprietor was Swedish immigrant William Birger Almen. Almen started his Beverly working career in 1913 as a machinist at the massive United Shoe Machinery Corporation on Elliott Street, where he at first was known by his middle name. Soon promoted to tool and diemaker, he was married in 1916 to Mimi (Mae) Jensen. What spurred him to switch from a steady paycheck at the "Shoe" to entrepreneur of a music store is not apparent (for a year or two he juggled both jobs, perhaps until he was sure his dream would work), but in 1923 he was open for business.

Ye Brunswick Music Shoppe was a shining beacon at the time when broadcast radio was coming into its own, and home record players, called "phonographs", were appearing in parlors everywhere. The store advertised that it sold "the best in long and short-wave radios," featuring the top brands – Zenith, Philco, RCA and Emerson. "Long wave" back then referred to the AM broadcast band.

For the record buying public, records meant the 10-inch, shellacked and very breakable 78 rpm version. The latest hits by the biggest stars of radio were for sale on the most popular labels – Brunswick, Decca, RCA Victor with its famous "His Master's Voice" emblem, and Melotone. For those who preferred to make their own music, the store sold drum kits, banjos, Gibson guitars and band instruments, and although not specifically mentioned, sheet music must have been available. The store even offered repair services. Lovers of music could meet their friends there, discuss the latest stuff with Mr. Almen, try things out and purchase what most appealed to them. For much of its lifetime, Ye Brunswick Music Shoppe had little or no competition at a time when Cabot Street was awash with choices for shoppers.

William Birman Almen died in 1953, and for a few years his widow, Mae, continued to operate the store. The mid-1950s was a time of revolution in music, with rock 'n' roll coming into its own, the 7-inch 45-rpm discs replacing the 78s, and long-playing albums made their debut. Top 40 radio stations and their popular DJs, could be heard on battery powered portable radios carried by teens to the beach. In 1957, Mae sold the business to William F. Hayes, who changed the name to Hayes Music Store. It was later taken over by Lawrence J. Hayes and moved to 250 Cabot St. Now only a few "old timers" can remember that quaint sign that beckoned music fans to Ye Brunswick Music Shoppe.

A version of this article appeared in the January 2015 e-newsletter of the Beverly Historical Society.

Power to the People
By Edward R. Brown

There was a time when Beverly residents enjoyed the luxury of having their own home town utility company, Beverly Gas and Electric. The company was organized in 1859 as the Beverly Gas Light Company, with $40,000 worth of stock and a plant on River Street near the railroad depot. It was combined in 1888 with the short-lived Beverly Electric Light Company, which was formed to bring the first incandescent power to town. Lights were turned on for the first time in July 1886, and Cabot Street was fully illuminated with street lights by March of 1887. The Beverly Farms *Advocate*, voice of the divisionist movement of the 1880s, complained that while downtown Beverly enjoyed electricity, Beverly Farms had to rely for illumination on "kerosene lamps and the Moon."

Beverly Gas and Electric boasted, in addition to its power plant and its own line and repair crews, an office and showroom building at 223 Cabot Street. Residents who wanted to update their kitchens with modern devices could buy what they needed and receive expert advice and installation, right on Cabot Street. An advertisement in the 1921 City Directory noted that the showroom offered a "complete line of gas and electric appliances." The firm's success was evident when the company president, Andrew N. Rogers, built an ornate mansion on Hale Street.

Of course, such a good thing could not last. By 1953 Beverly Gas and Electric was history, replaced at the Cabot Street location by two firms, North Shore Gas Company and Essex County Electric Company, which said it was "part of the New England Electric system." The showroom remained open. Merger mania continued, and by the 1970s the firm was called Boston Gas and Massachusetts Electric Company. Today, both forms of power are provided by the super-utility, National

Grid. The lovely Renaissance-style building at 223 Cabot was torn down in 1976, a victim of changing times.

A version of this article appeared in January 2015 e-newsletter of the Beverly Historical Society.

Shopping in the Land of Nostalgia
By Gail Balentine

Each year, when it's time to dig out my spring clothes and decide what I need to buy for the season, I feel dread. This is because the number of places I have to go or search for online to find the correct color, style and size feels overwhelming. I try to start out in an optimistic frame of mind, but invariably end up with a headache, often willing to settle for a piece of clothing or spending more money than I should, just to end the painful process.

Thinking about the ordeal can easily bring on a wave of nostalgia for downtown Beverly and the Cabot Street of the 1950s and 1960s with its family-oriented stores. Located within three or four blocks, it was easy to shop downtown by walking there, taking a bus or driving your car and parking in one convenient spot.

You could start at Alcon's, on the corner of Washington and Cabot, where there were shoes for the whole family – Mary Janes, saddle shoes, penny loafers, pumps, or wingtips. The salesmen took pride in making sure the shoes fit, with room for a child's foot to grow.

Then you could go on to department stores, Almy, Bigelow & Washburn, known simply as Almy's, across the street from the YMCA, and Webber's, on the corner of Broadway and Cabot. The sales-ladies knew their inventory and could estimate your size with one quick look; they often made helpful suggestions about what looked good and what was appropriate to wear for certain events. Ship n'Shore blouses, Pandora sweaters, Pendleton skirts and other brand name clothes lined shelves and filled racks. They came in mostly "basic" colors – black,

Almy's is shown on the right of Cabot Street across from the YMCA, early 1960s.

navy, tan or white for skirts and pants (many with matching sweaters) and pastels and stripes for blouses. Clothes lasted for more than one season, so when you went back the next year, you could purchase a new top or accessory to match what you already had, thereby building a wardrobe.

If you or your child played sports, just another few minutes' walk past Almy's would bring you to Cor-Nix Rubber Company, located on the corner of Pond and Cabot Streets. Here you could supply all your needs for sports clothing and equipment.

It could be a trick of time, but it seemed whatever I needed, I found within these few stores, in a short period of time and at a reasonable price. I know, as the saying goes, "you can't go home again", but that doesn't stop my memories – maybe it even enhances them.

A version of this article appeared in the March 2016 e-newsletter of the Beverly Historical Society

Chapter 7: Colorful Characters

Dorcas Hoar: Beverly's Resident 'Witch'
By Edward R. Brown

She was perhaps the most colorful Beverly resident of the 17th century, although with a decidedly malignant side, and she was the only resident of this town to be condemned for witchcraft during the infamous trials of 1692. She was Dorcas Hoar, whose home stood on the far western part of what is now Central Cemetery. It was demolished early in the 20th century, but a photo survives in the collection of Historic Beverly.

Born Dorcas Galley, daughter of John Galley of Salem, she was the wife of William Hoar, a fisherman by trade, who was living on the Bass River Side, (Beverly) by 1651. They had eight children. Dorcas first came to public attention in 1678, when she was the town's leading receiver of stolen goods, a sort of female version of Dickens's Fagin. She used several of her own children in the pursuit of other people's property, along with the servants of other townspeople. One of those was the vicious Margaret Lord, the teenage live-in maid of the Reverend John Hale and his first wife, Rebecca. Margaret stole whatever she could from the parsonage, taking it all down the street to her friend Dorcas Hoar. The minister and his wife were at first not aware of the missing property, but their children, Becky, then 12, and Robert, 9, who often were left in the care of the servants while their parents were abroad on ministerial duties, knew very well of the thefts by Lord and various of the Hoar children. Lord cowed them into silence with, among other threats, that since they knew Dorcas Hoar was a witch, she would use her powers to hurt them. Once the thefts came to light, Dorcas and three of her daughters, two of them married, went before the Quarter Court to answer charges of receiving stolen goods. They got off lightly, but some of the Hoar children took revenge on John Hale by beating his cows, one of them fatally, an act Beverly's first minister accepted with Christian charity.

Dorcas at the time had another money-making sideline. That was by telling fortunes, something no respectable person would do in the 17th century since it was considered a form of witchcraft. She had somehow obtained a book on palm reading and used it to her advantage. When Reverend Hale found out about it he warned her that it was "an evil book and an evil art." She promised to desist but of course was lying. Word of her misdeeds was clearly known in the community. In 1690 David Balch, a 19-year-old, suffering from a fatal illness, told a witness he could see a "confederacy" of witches at the head of his bed, one of whom was Goodwife Hoar.

Dorcas Hoar's house stood on Hale Street, now part of Central Cemetery.

With her well-earned reputation, it is no surprise that Dorcas was one of the first called out by the Salem Village (Danvers) accusers when the delusion of 1692 broke out. She was arraigned, indicted, tried, convicted and sentence to death by the witch court despite her earlier protestations of innocence against her accusers at her arraignment: "Oh! You are liars, and God will stop the mouth of liars!" Dorcas was to be hanged at Salem on September 22, 1692 along with eight other victims of the tragedy in the last executions carried out before Governor Phips dissolved the witch court and people began to realize how wrong they had been. The day before her scheduled execution Dorcas saved herself by playing her last card. Since only those who insisted on their innocence were killed, Dorcas made an elaborate confession in the jail before the magistrates and ministers, including John Hale. She added a touch of realism by exhibiting a scar which she claimed to have received from someone she had afflicted.

An express rider was sent to Boston with a letter to the governor seeking a reprieve for her, and a thirty-day respite from the sentence was granted. Samuel Sewall, one of the judges of the special court, wrote in his diary that night about Dorcas Hoar: "An order is sent to the sheriff to forbear her execution, notwithstanding her being in the warrant to die tomorrow. This is the first convicted witch who has confessed." The next day the other eight victims boarded the cart bound for the gallows, but Dorcas stayed behind. The short reprieve was enough, since no more convicted witches would die, and Dorcas regained her freedom when the jails were cleared in 1693. John Hale in his book *A Modest Enquiry into the Nature of Witchcraft* mentioned Dorcas, referring to her as "D.H."

The rest of her life was spent in relative anonymity. While she had claimed to tell her own fortune and had told others she would "live better" after her husband died, as a convicted and "outlawed" felon she received no bequest from William Hoar's estate. While no evidence exists, it is likely that most people in town would have shunned her. By 1699 she was a pauper, supported by the taxpayers. Records show that she was fortunate at least to be "farmed out" to her married daughter Annis (Nancy), who was married to William King Jr. of Salem. The agreement signed by the Beverly selectmen with William King Jr. called for the town to pay four pounds in money a year for Dorcas's upkeep. The agreement was renewed in 1704, but since the clerks didn't bother to record the deaths of paupers, the date of her death does not appear in the vital records, and her place of burial is unknown. It must have been a bitter last few years on earth for someone who had lived such a colorful life.

A version of this article appeared in the June 2018 e-newsletter of Historic Beverly.

Infamous Elopement

By Stephen P. Hall

We are all familiar with the Hollywood version of an elopement. The young and anxious groom sneaks up to the home of his prospective bride, places a ladder under her window and pelts it with small pebbles to get her attention. Quickly the couple make their escape. However, in the 18th century the legal definition of elopement was quite different. Law books defined it as, "…the departure of a married woman from her husband and dwelling with an adulterer." The law goes on to state that no matter how bad her conduct, if she stays with her husband,

"…he is bound to provide her with necessaries…but when she elopes, the husband is no longer liable for her alimony, and is not bound to pay debts…when the separation is notorious…." And it further warns anyone who gives her credit under these circumstances, does so at his peril.

Examples of this type of elopement can be found in the newspapers of the 18th and 19th centuries. One such notice was published in the September 16, 1771 issue of the *Essex Gazette*, by Josiah Woodbury of Beverly. It reads:

"Ran away from Josiah Woodbury, Cooper, his House Plague for 7 long years, Masury Old Moll, alias Trial of Vengeance. He that lost will never seek her; he that shall keep her, I will give a Bushel of Beans. I forwarn all persons in Town or Country from trusting said Trial of Vengeance. I have hove all the old shoes I can for joy; and all my neighbours rejoice with me: A good Riddance of bad Ware. Amen. Josiah Woodbury."

Although many notices in the newspapers of the time started with the phrase "Ran away" they usually were notices of runaway slaves. A slave master would have had better regard for his valuable property, and would have requested help in locating her, rather than the admonishment and good riddance attitude displayed by Mr. Woodbury. Clearly this was a public comment regarding the actions of his wife and how he felt about her. In a small town like Beverly in the 18th century this must have been quite remarkable – and kept the town talking. The news of the elopement made it likely that the runaway couple would have had trouble finding shelter and support in the community.

A bit of genealogical detective work revealed that Josiah Woodbury was born in 1709, the son of Josiah and Lydia (Herrick) Woodbury. He was the great grandson of one of Beverly's earliest settlers, Old Planter John Woodbury. Josiah's first wife was Hannah Perkins of Ipswich. They married in 1731 and had eight children that survived to maturity and three others that died young. This appears to have been a happy marriage that came to a sudden end with her death in June 1761, when she was 46.

Josiah, suddenly adrift without Hannah, and with at least three minor children to care for, ended his mourning period in December 1764 when he married Mary Masurey of Salem. "Moll" is often a nickname for Mary, so it appears that Mary Masurey is the person he is complaining about in his colorful newspaper listing. It is unclear if Masurey is her maiden name or if she was a widow. The phrase *"She has been a plague for seven years"* makes it transparently clear that the second marriage of Josiah Woodbury was unhappy from the start. The references to *"heaving old shoes* and *"he that shall keep her..."* indicates that she eloped with another man and did not just run off on her own.

Just two years later, in 1773, Woodbury joined his beloved first wife, Hannah in the next grave at Second Parish Cemetery in North Beverly. They are still there, side by side, their tombstones joined together in eternal embrace. Somehow, I suspect that after his unhappy marriage to *"Old Moll, alias Trial of Vengeance"* he was happy to shed his mortal coil and spend eternity next to Hannah, mother of all his children and his happy companion.

A version of this article appeared in the 2007 Beverly Historical Society's *Chronicle*.

Attention, Industry, Duty: Nathan Dane
By Terri McFadden

Although not well-remembered today, Nathan Dane (1752-1835) was an important and influential law maker in the early days of the Republic. He is credited with writing the one of the most important pieces of legislation to come out of the Articles of Confederation period, the Northwest Ordinance of 1787. Without this law American history may have taken quite a different course.

Dane was born in Ipswich, Massachusetts in 1752, the son of Daniel and Abigail Dane. He attended the local primary school and, until age 20, worked on his father's farm. As a young man he decided to prepare himself for college. In a mere eight months he had read all the

Nathan Dane was a lawyer, legislator and author of the first systematic examination of American law. Portrait by Chester Harding about 1833.

books necessary for admission. In 1778 he graduated with honors from Harvard College and began to "read law" with Judge William Wetmore of Salem. After admission to the bar, Dane set up a law practice in Beverly. His political career was launched soon after and he served in many capacities including in both the Massachusetts House of Representatives and Senate, as a member of the Continental Congress and as a judge of the Court of Common Pleas for Essex County.

In 1786 the area west of the Ohio River was the American frontier and the first states to enter the union, outside of the original thirteen, were carved from this region. Congress had to decide how the area would be divided, how future states would enter the union, and how they would be governed. Dane served on the committee charged with writing this legislation and was the chief author of the law. Its principal provisions included the number of states that could be formed – not less than three nor more than five – a three stage method for admitting new states and a bill of rights protecting religious freedom, the right to a writ of habeas corpus, and trial by jury. In a 1787 letter to his colleague Rufus King, Dane wrote that the last article in the ordinance, prohibiting slavery, was a last-minute addition, which he hadn't expected to pass. This article may have ensured the course of the Civil War. Eventually five new states were carved out of the territory: Ohio, Indiana, Illinois, Michigan, and Wisconsin. Looking at a map of the country just prior to Civil War, it is possible to envision this huge area as slave-holding states, tipping the balance of the war in favor of the Confederacy.

Dane understood the need to amend the Articles of Confederation, which were far too weak to provide a successful government for the new country. In one letter he wrote about the areas that needed to be addressed, among them impost taxes, the sale of Federal lands, making treaties with foreign powers, as well as the need for Congress to have power over commerce. All of these topics were eventually addressed by the U.S. Constitution.

At first glance there are two events in Dane's career that seem at odds with this thoughtful, dutiful and dedicated public servant. He opposed the final draft of the Constitution and he attended the Hartford Convention. The Hartford Convention of 1814 was a meeting of New England Federalists who saw the policies of the Jefferson and Madison administrations as disastrous to the commercial and political life of New England. There was talk as early as 1809 about New England seceding from Union and this was rumored to be a topic addressed at the Convention. Although Dane's reputation suffered as a result of his attendance, he wrote that he was there to "prevent mischief." The proposals that came out of the Hartford Convention dealt with balancing power between the states, limits on presidential terms, and the length of future embargos. There was no proposal drafted to form a new country. Perhaps the sober leadership of Nathan Dane did indeed prevent mischief.

His opposition to the Constitution as originally written isn't hard to understand. For his entire career he had championed rights for the common citizen. As it was ratified in 1788, the Constitution lacked a bill of rights. It wasn't until 1789, when the first ten amendments were adopted, that Dane felt the civil rights of American citizens were safeguarded.

In a letter of 1787 he commented on his fellow law makers: "Many gentlemen appear to attend [Congress] only as it suits their private concerns; this never can answer the purpose in the administration of a Government where great attention and industry is required to understand its parts...." There is no doubt that Nathan Dane gave his attention and industry to doing his duty – our country is better off for those efforts.

A version of this article appeared in the Winter 2013 issue of the *Chronicle*.

The Curious Case of Hale Hilton
By Terri McFadden

We traveled a circuitous route to discover the story of Hale Hilton (1759-1841), at various times in his life a musician, yeoman, captain and merchant. In the course of the research we found a larger American story.

His name first came up as we learned about the tenant farmers of Hale Farm, the 17th century home of Reverend John Hale. Hilton was the first of these tenant farmers. No relation to the minister, he was named after his mother's brother, Hale Thorndike. Hilton and his wife lived at Hale Farm from 1782 to 1793 – the part of his career in which he was described as a yeoman or farmer. During this period, he was also pursuing maritime activities. Records show he was the captain of the schooner *Betsey* in 1787.

Hale Hilton was born in 1759, the youngest of six children of John and Judith (Thorndike) Hilton. He was a cousin and contemporary of Israel Thorndike, Beverly's first millionaire. Thorndike enters our story several times.

During the American Revolution Hilton served for a year and a half in Captain John Low's company in the 19th Regiment as a fifer. In 1777 for another six months he was a seaman aboard the privateer *Tyrannicide*. He was a sea captain in 1783 when he married his first wife Elizabeth Leech. In 1793 Hale and Elizabeth purchased a house on Bartlett Street from his cousin Israel Thorndike for 190 pounds.

It seems evident, even from the relatively small paper trail uncovered, that Captain Hilton was an ambitious, but not necessarily prudent, man. The first evidence of this is a large loan that he took from his father-in-law, Nathan Leech, in May 1797 in the amount of $1667.97. In September of that year Hilton purchased the brig *Pilgrim* for $2,300. One of the four owners who sold the vessel was Israel Thorndike. An investment so large was normally shared. The idea was to minimize risk, while retaining a large share of the profits. Hale Hilton ignored this basic idea and took a chance, likely hoping to make his fortune. It proved his undoing.

Two events on the larger world stage converged with Hale Hilton's quest to become a wealthy merchant. The first was the discovery by Captain Jonathan Carnes of Salem, of a port in Sumatra where it was possible to purchase the incredibly valuable crop of pepper directly from the growers. Carnes sailed from Salem in December 1795, returning two years later. The owners and investors of the *Rajah* realized an astounding 700% profit on their investment. They sold some of the cargo to other ship owners, evidently including Hale Hilton. His brig, the *Pilgrim* sailed out of port with a cargo of pepper and other goods, bound across the Atlantic. It was off the coast of France that the second event conspired to ruin Hilton. French privateers captured the vessel, taking her to isle Saint Jean de Luz late in 1797, one of the earliest actions in a little-known, undeclared war with France called the Quasi-War.

The Quasi-War (officially dated 1798-1800) involved the Jay Treaty of 1794 made with Great Britain. The French saw this as America turning away from our alliance with them. In addition, after the French Revolution, the American government refused to pay debts incurred to the French crown during the American Revolution, asserting the money had been loaned by a government which no longer existed. Soon French privateers began seizing American vessels which were trading with the British. Hundreds of ships were captured, among them Hilton's *Pilgrim*. Within months Hale Hilton began his quest to recover his lost fortune – first through insurance claims and later through the U.S. government "spoliations" claims. Neither effort was successful. Eventually Hilton was forced to declare bankruptcy. In June of 1801 the sheriff of Essex County was asked to attach his goods and estate. Hilton had borrowed money from Israel Thorndike in the amount of $3000, which he had failed to repay. Other law suits were filed for money he owed.

A few months later his former father-in-law Nathan Leech (Hilton's wife Elizabeth had died in 1799) pled with "with tears" in his eyes for help for Hale. Leech arranged with William Gray, Jr., to settle Hilton's affairs, take his property and pay his debts.

For more than 40 years Hale Hilton continued his quest for redress for the loss of his ship and its cargo of pepper. He remarried in 1800 to a woman named Elizabeth Dennis. In his will of 1840 he stated that he gave her all his real and personal estate "...that I die possessed of and the property that may be recovered for my loss of the Brig *Pilgrim* and her cargo." The inventory following his death in 1841 lists his personal and real estate at a total of $510.50, a pittance for a man who had hoped to become a merchant prince. The contrast to his cousin, Israel Thorndike who died in 1833, couldn't be greater. Thorndike's personal estate alone was listed as $909,928.02. Hilton's failures where his cousin succeeded so spectacularly must surely have rankled. Perhaps the lesson we can draw from the story of Hale Hilton is that financial success is a combination of daring, prudence, and luck. With less of the first ingredient or more of the second and third, the story of Hale Hilton might have had quite a different ending.

Israel Thorndike was a cousin of Hale Hilton.

A version of this article appeared in the Winter 2014 issue of the *Chronicle*.

Thomas Barrett: Fifty Years a Church Sexton
By Terri McFadden

Born in Newport, Rhode Island in 1759, Thomas Barrett moved as a young man to Beverly where he soon began his life's work. He served Beverly's First Parish Church as its sexton for more than fifty years. Although not as important today, the office of sexton was of great importance in churches of the past. His duties included maintaining church property, ringing the bells for service and the "passing bell" in honor of the dead. He was also required to turn the hour glass during the sermon, sometimes as many as three times during the morning service. Thomas Barrett was, according to Reverend Christopher Thayer, "...ever so orderly and punctual, so respectful and reverential, so thoughtful and kind toward the living, so tender of the dead." Barrett's granddaughter, poet Lucy Larcom, wrote about getting locked in the bell-tower of the church, and being overjoyed when rescued by the "two beloved human faces" – her father and grandfather.

Gravestone of Lois Barrett, wife of Thomas Barrett; she died in 1796.

His personal life was not quite as smooth as his work life. He married Lois Symonds of Salem and the couple had four children between 1786 and 1789. The last two were twin girls. Sadly, Lois died soon after the birth, age just 29 – likely of an infection as a result of childbirth. Thomas married two more times; to Lydia Smith in 1818 and to Sarah Smith in 1840. When Thomas died at age 87 in April 1846, he was buried next to Lois, "the wife of his youth" – the last burial in the ancient burial ground, today called the Abbott Street Cemetery.

A version of this article appeared in the April 2015 e-newsletter of the Beverly Historical Society.

Andrew Preston Peabody: A life well lived
By Terri McFadden

Andrew P. Peabody (1811-1893) was a teacher, minister, and Harvard professor.

Historical tales come to us in many ways, often unexpectedly. Once one of our volunteers shared a story he'd read while organizing some of our 19th century documents. It was the intriguing account of a child, Andrew Preston Peabody, who had the unusual ability to read in the normal way but who could also read upside down! Although I'd never heard this story, the name rang a bell. In fact, Andrew Preston Peabody, born in Beverly in 1811, was the son of Andrew and Polly (Rantoul) Peabody, and the nephew of Robert Rantoul, Sr.

As the youngest pupil in a Dame School, the teacher pinned the boy by his sleeve to her clothing, perhaps to keep him from wandering off. While the other children recited their lessons, the teacher kept the textbook open on her lap. Andrew learned to read upside down before he learned the normal way. He was remarkable in other ways as well, starting Harvard College at the tender age of 12 and graduating at 15; one of the youngest students in that institution's history to get a bachelor's degree.

Later in life he stated that his "profession as a clergyman was determined" at birth. His father, on his deathbed, made his wife promise to guide the then three-year-old to that career. Between his mother and Reverend Abiel Abbot, minister of Beverly's First Parish church, the boy was indeed moved in that direction. However, for the first seven years after leaving Harvard he taught school, only later becoming ordained. He took up his first ministerial post in Portsmouth, New

Hampshire, but just two weeks later the senior pastor died suddenly and the young man was forced to take responsibility for the entire parish. He ministered to the South Parish congregation for the next 28 years.

He and his large family then moved to Cambridge, Massachusetts, where Dr. Peabody became Harvard's preacher and a counselor and advisor to generations of undergraduates. He was a popular lecturer and held the position of Plummer Professor of Morals and Ethics, wrote numerous books and served as the editor of the North American Review. He was known to say that each person should have a vocation and several avocations. His life story suggests that he followed this excellent advice. He died just a few days short of his 82nd birthday.

A version of this article appeared in the April 2017 e-newsletter of the Beverly Historical Society.

Broadway Ladies

By Edward R. Brown

Two of the many beautiful houses on Broadway, Beverly's "showplace" street of the late 1800s, were owned by two very talented and unusual women.

Number 12 Broadway, built in 1884, was the home of Sarah Warner Clark, one of Beverly's most active community volunteers of her time. Born in 1839, she was the daughter of successful businessman and politician Augustus N. Clark and his wife Hitty, whose home was nearby at 19 Broadway. Among Miss Clark's many accomplishments was to serve as president of the Women's Foreign Missionary Society of the Dane Street Church, treasurer of the Essex Branch of the Women's Benevolent Association, and as a member of the Beverly Hospital Corporation. She also was active in the Beverly Female Charitable Society and the Beverly Historical Society, to which she gave a large imported Asian vase. In addition, she formed and for 25 years was the superintendent of the Dane Street Church Sunday School. When plans were launched to build a new YMCA on Cabot Street, she made a major donation to the building campaign. Miss Clark died June 28, 1914.

Looking west on Broadway in the 1880s.

Mrs. Harriet E. Jenness, better known locally as Hattie, lived at number 34; her talent was in the shoemaking business. Her Victorian house was built in 1885, possibly by her husband John, who was a carpenter. In 1893 Hattie Jenness was forewoman of a shoe factory in West Lynn. She was a strong-willed woman, able to handle even the toughest male employees. She and her husband used their large home as a lodging house with as many as ten lodgers boarding with them. Interestingly, she was listed in the U.S. Census record of 1900 as the head of the household and she, not her husband, was the purchaser of the property where her home was built; a rather unusual situation for a married woman of that time.

Eventually Harriet went into business for herself here in Beverly. She was a "contract stitcher," with a business address on Bow Street, serving as backup to this city's many shoe factories. Often one of the factories would receive a large order with a quick turnaround date. Faced with the possibility of having to add an extra shift, the factory brass would turn to Hattie. Using plans and materials supplied by the contractor, Hattie called her crew together and they completed the order. Hattie put some of her profits into her home. On August 20, 1892, the *Beverly Citizen* reported: "The residence of Mrs. Hattie Jenness on Broadway is being enlarged and much improved. A piazza will be built on the front of the house, adding greatly to its appearance."

A version of this article appeared in the April 2015 e-newsletter of the Beverly Historical Society.

Alice Blue Gown Invades Beverly
By Stephen P. Hall

In 1904 all the tongues up and down the North Shore were wagging wildly as "Alice Blue Gown" descended upon the people of Beverly. The 20-year-old daughter of President Teddy Roosevelt, Alice Lee Roosevelt was being courted by Nicholas Longworth, Jr., congressman of Ohio and one of the country's most eligible bachelors.

At first her family believed there was a little game going on between Alice and her best friend, Marguerite Cassini, daughter of the Russian ambassador, to see who could capture the congressman's attention. Sometimes Congressman Longworth would be spotted with Alice and sometimes it was Marguerite on his arm. However, it soon became apparent to First Lady Edith Roosevelt that it was no game for her stepdaughter Alice. She had fallen in love with Nick Longworth, who was some 15 years her senior.

The turning point in their relationship appears to have occurred when President Roosevelt sent his Secretary of War, William Howard Taft on a trip to the far east, along with several members of Congress and Alice Roosevelt – serving as her father's official representative. While on this junket she literally made a big splash by jumping into the ship's swimming pool fully dressed. Taft felt it his duty to act as chaperone to Miss Roosevelt. He determined that she and Nicolas Longworth had become much too friendly and pulled Alice aside with a pointed question. Was she engaged to Congressman Longworth? "More or less, Mr. Secretary." she answered, "More or less." A few months later, on February 17, 1906, Alice Roosevelt wed the Ohio congressman.

Alice's widowed mother-in-law, Susan Walker Longworth, had built a mansion on Hale Street in Beverly in 1897, overlooking beautiful Mingo Beach. This provided a summer home from which Alice and her husband would "scorch" down the local dirt roads with their wild companions. She was known for driving around town in her "electric," poking convention in the eye and looking for a midnight party. Her assaults on the sleeping townsfolk were called "Night Riders" raids; named after the infamous Tennessee vigilantes.

Longworth House at 357 Hale Street. Built in 1897, the house remained in the family until the 1930s.

Leading her gang of raiders to the summer estates, Alice Roosevelt Longworth would position herself outside the bedroom window of potential party recruits, issuing "cat calls and howling" until she roused the victim. She would not leave until she had taken someone in tow, and then off she headed to the next summer residence. A military aide to President Roosevelt wrote, "Now the highest social honor one can have is a raid from the Night Raiders led by the intrepid Alice." The dust would fly behind them as they picked up other like-minded affluent party goers from the summer 'cottages' of Beverly Farms, Prides Crossing, and the Cove. One man reported that she "invites those who visited her in their motor car to have some tea and lemonade…and if they accept the latter they are surprised to find a delicious gin fizz…."

Her father was by this time used to the wacky antics of his oldest child. He knew she enjoyed shocking people, in fact she made a lifetime career out of her outrageous behavior. Famously, President Roosevelt said that, "he could manage the government or manage Alice, but couldn't possibly do both at once."

Her popularity was undisputed. When it was discovered that a particular gray-blue was her favorite color, "Alice blue" was born.

Sheet music for the hit song *Alice Blue Gown* became almost impossible to find, quickly selling out at the music stores. By the standards of the day, Alice was wild indeed, and she was famous for her one-liners. About her father she quipped, "He wanted to be the bride at every wedding and the corpse at every funeral." Apparently, the apple didn't fall too far from the tree!

She also got her spirit of adventure from her father. She loved automobiles and set speed records in a friend's roadster. It was said that her devilish smile could raise welts on the backs of the necks of the folks nearest to her at the dinner table, and her tongue-lashings regularly drew blood. The wide-brimmed hats, popular in Alice's youth, became her signature style and she wore them most of her long life. In 1965 she told President Lyndon Johnson that she wore a hat so that he couldn't get close enough to kiss her. Her high-jinx in Beverly came to an end about 1917 and she spent the next 60 years tormenting and amusing the citizens of Washington, D.C.

Well into her nineties she reflected on her life: "…having graduated from being considered rather a loathsome combination of Marie Dressler and Phyllis Diller, I seem to have achieved a symbolism of sort in my dotage. Rather like Queen Victoria, I fear [but] hopefully with more levity." She often said that her philosophy of life was simple. "Fill what's empty. Empty what's full. And scratch where it itches." She was truly one of a kind.

A version of this article appeared in the Winter 2006 issue of the *Chronicle*.

Public Service and Civic Duty

By Susan Milstein

Among the earliest summer residents of Beverly were the Loring Family. Charles Greeley Loring (1794-1867), built a summer home on the coast in 1846. Six years later, in 1852 attorney Caleb William Loring (1819-1897) built his family summer home in Pride's Crossing on land owned by his father. He named the home "Burn Side." By 1869 Caleb and his children were making Burn Side their year-round residence. His daughters Katharine (1849-1943) and her sister Louisa (1854-1924) resided in their Beverly home for much of their lives. It was a stroke of luck for Beverly that this became their home.

The Loring family had long had a tradition of giving back to the community at large, the four children of Caleb Loring continued this work. William (1851-1930) became the Assistant Attorney General of Massachusetts and served for many years as an Associate Justice of the Supreme Judicial Court. His brother Augustus (1857-1938) was a lawyer, two term state senator and trustee of the Smithsonian.

Katharine (top) and Louisa Loring

Although Katharine Loring and her younger sister, Louisa lived during a time when women had few professional opportunities, they nevertheless made their mark on many institutions. Both women lived busy and productive lives, giving countless hours to many organizations. One major focus of Katharine's energy was the Beverly Historical Society where she served as president for 23 years, from 1918 to 1941. During her tenure the Society acquired its two additional properties, Balch House and Hale Farm. Katharine helped furnish Hale Farm with the gift of a lovely c. 1820 set of bedroom furniture, displayed in the large bedroom on the second floor. During her lifetime, Loring donated many books and pamphlets related to the history of Beverly, Salem and other parts of Essex County. She contributed a group of early printed sermons from the First Parish Church in Beverly, dating between 1773 and 1870.

Both Katharine and Louisa Loring were involved in other local causes as well. Katharine tended toward education causes and Louisa toward improving lives by improving health. Katharine was on the board of the Beverly Public Library for many years and she donated the land where the Beverly Farms branch of the library stands. She was a founding member of the Society to Encourage Studies at Home and the Saturday Morning Club. Both organizations were aimed at improving the education and intellectual growth in women. Her friend, Alice James wrote: "There is nothing she cannot do from hewing wood and drawing water to driving runaway horses to educating every woman in America." Louisa was a great supporter of the Red Cross, participating in life-saving drills. She was a member of the Anti-Tuberculosis Society of Beverly and a director of Beverly Hospital. She also helped found a sanitarium in South Carolina. Both Louisa and her sister assisted with relief work following the terrible Salem fire of 1914. Their devotion to public service remains an inspiration. The world in general and Beverly in particular are better because of their common sense of duty.

A version of this article appeared in the Fall 2015 Chronicle.

Sculpture in War and Peace
By Terri McFadden

The career of artist Anna Coleman (Watts) Ladd (1878-1939) is both interesting and unexpected. She was born to a well-to-do couple in Bryn Mawr, Pennsylvania. Her father, John Watts, was a successful attorney. When she was quite young she decided to become a sculptor, one of the few professions considered acceptable for women at the time. She traveled to Europe, studying in Rome and Paris. On her return young Anna continued her training at the Boston Museum School with Bela Lyon Pratt, of the first art teachers in the nation to train women. Following her studies, she received many commissions.

In 1905 she married Boston physician Maynard Ladd. The couple lived on Clarendon Street in Boston, summering on the North Shore, first in Manchester and after the First World War in Beverly Farms.

Her goals in the early part of her career were "to work for all outdoors, to produce sculpture to be placed on street corners, on walks, on open roads [and] to express the joy and youth and dreams of human nature." *Triton Babies*, one of her most famous works, does just that. First exhibited at the San Francisco Panama-Pacific Exposition in 1915, this exuberant sculpture of two children playing was placed in Boston Public Garden in 1922; in 1924 it was moved to its current location near Charles Street.

Many of her pieces explored themes of mythological characters and themes. *Wind and Spray* depicts young, nude males and females dancing in a ring of waves. When it was displayed in Boston, it caused something of a furor and was withdrawn from view. Evidently, showing naked children was acceptable because *Triton Babies* was popular with the public from the beginning. In 1916 Ladd held a one-woman show in Boston where she exhibited more than 40 works, described as "garden and fountain bronzes." She also exhibited in San Francisco, Philadelphia, New York, and Washington D.C.

In addition to bronze, Ladd worked in marble and produced bas-relief sculptures and medallions. She sculpted likenesses of many famous people of her day, including the ballet dancer Anna Pavlova, actress Ethel Barrymore and aviator Charles Lindbergh. A nude called *Water Sprite*, was reportedly modeled after actress Bette Davis. A woman of many talents, Anna Ladd wrote two novels and several plays.

One of her plays, about a sculptress who went to war, was based on her own experiences during World War I. Late in 1917, she and her husband traveled to France where Dr. Ladd established a hospital for children near the front line. About this time Anna heard of a British artist, Francis Wood, who had begun making metal masks for soldiers so disfigured from wounds that plastic surgery could do nothing for them. After consulting with Wood, Ladd opened the Studio for Portrait Masks in Paris, funded by the American Red Cross and run by Ladd.

To create a mask a plaster cast was taken of the injured soldier's face. Plasticine or clay was applied to the inside of the cast to create a positive impression and to fill in any missing parts. Next, using photographs, Ladd and her assistants sculpted the man's original features from a sheet of galvanized copper. Finally, it was painted with enamel to match the skin tone. Some masks covered the whole face, others just the damaged area, but all were life-changing for those terribly damaged men. For her work she awarded the Legion d'Honneur Croix de Chevalier and the Serbian Order of Saint Sava.

World War I memorial Cost of Victory, in the Beverly Farms Cemetery, sculpted by Anna Coleman Ladd.

Following her return to the United States, Anna Ladd began working in her Preston Place home in Beverly Farms. In her studio, called "Arden" she produced works dramatically different from the lighthearted pieces made before the war. Her marble World War I memorial *Cost of Victory* stands in the Beverly Farms cemetery, the centerpiece for the American Legion lot. Another commission for the American Legion in Manchester, Massachusetts is a bronze two-sided plaque. One side, *Night*, shows a dead soldier caught on barbed wire; the reverse, *Dawn* shows a man being raised above the battlefield by an angel. The theme of hope of life after death is one she returned to often.

Ladd wrote: "Peace is not represented as woman with a dove and olive branch, but as the only power capable of crushing and controlling the brute, War...." Her impressive legacy survives in numerous art works both somber and charming, and in the memory of the men she was able to help regain a semblance of a normal life.

A version of this article appeared in the Beverly Historical Society Spring 2016 *Chronicle*.

Otis Dunham and his Castle
By Terri McFadden

Born in Beverly in 1876, Otis Dunham lived most of his life here. Although he started his career as an attorney, early on he joined the candy manufacturer of Page & Shaw of Cambridge, becoming the manager. In 1919 Dunham purchased the company, expanding the company internationally, establishing candy stores in England and France, and building a large factory in Canada. All of these events are part of an ordinary story of a successful businessman. But what is interesting about Dunham was what he did with his money at his Beverly estate "off Brimbal" as the city directories gave his address for nearly 50 years.

He named the place that he and his family lived in "Lodge Pole Ranch", but it was called Dunham Castle by locals. The architecture of the building was reportedly inspired by French chateaus. But more than European locales, Otis Dunham was greatly enamored of the American West. In some photographs he is pictured in full Plains Indian headdress, feeding his pet reindeer on the steps of his Beverly home. He brought cowboys and members of the Blackfoot tribe to Beverly to live for a time and reportedly kept a flock of sheep on the property as well as several buffalo. In addition, on a flat roof of the home, Dunham constructed a "midget" golf course and on others roof gardens flourished.

There are several indications that Otis Dunham had some financial problems during the Great Depression. The federal government put a lien on his property for non-payment of taxes in the early 1930s. However, he paid his debt and lived at Lodge Pole Ranch until the late 1940s, when he moved to California. Not long after Dunham Road was named and during the early 1950s it was developed for homes. Otis's castle, for a short time, became a restaurant called Chateau Montserrat and later the home of Amerac microwave equipment. In 1955 the new "Music Tent" opened its doors on a part of the former Lodge Pole Ranch property; the North Shore Music Theater has called the place home ever since, continuing the entertaining tradition of Otis Emerson Dunham.

A version of this article appeared in the April 2016 e-newsletter of the Beverly Historical Society.

Contributing to Science and Nature
By Terri McFadden

Over the centuries Beverly residents have participated in many ways on the national and world stage in political, cultural and scientific endeavors. In the field of zoology and conservation one man's contributions still resonate. His name was Harold Jefferson Coolidge, Jr. who was born in 1904 in Boston. Coolidge was a long-time summer resident of Beverly, living for many years in the Cove and Centerville. He attended the University of Arizona where he obtained his undergraduate degree. Although he thought of becoming a diplomat, his interest turned to zoology and he got his graduate degree in that field from Harvard College, specializing in primatology.

In the 1920s and 1930s Coolidge participated in several important expeditions. The most important to his work focused on the study of primates, the first to Africa and two others to Asia. Coolidge revised the genus Gorilla and later published the first detailed account of bonobos, also called pigmy chimpanzees. At the time these animals were thought to be the same species as the common chimp. Coolidge recognized their differences and elevated them to species rank, Pan paniscus. The Asian primates collected by Coolidge remain one of the more important collections of mammals in the Harvard collection at the Museum of Comparative Zoology (MCZ). Unusual for the time, Coolidge took careful and detailed data, including weight and measurements, for each animal captured for study. Coolidge became a curator of mammalogy at the MCZ.

During World War II he served in the OSS gaining the rank of major. Along with his assistant Julia Williams (later the famous chef, Julia Child) Coolidge developed a chemical shark repellent. This mixture was cooked up in a bathtub according to Child and kept sharks away from military personnel awaiting rescue in the water for up to eight hours. In 1945 Coolidge was awarded the Legion of Merit for his work.

The house at 38 Standley Street was the summer home of Harold Coolidge and his family.

Recognizing the need to preserve wildlife as well as the environment, in later years Coolidge helped found several important conservation organizations. He was a member of the U.S. delegation to the Fontainebleau conference where the International Union for the Conservation of Nature (IUCN) was founded, was a founding member of the World Wildlife Fund (WWF) and served on the WWF board. Over the course of his decades-long career he received many awards, including the J. Paul Getty wildlife prize for conservation. President Jimmy Carter, giving the award to Coolidge said, "You gave very early warning of the plight of endangered species when few could even comprehend this concept."

In February 1985, just past his 81st birthday, Harold J. Coolidge fell at his Beverly home and died shortly afterwards, from complications as a result of the fall. As a descendent of President Thomas Jefferson, he was buried in the private family cemetery at Monticello. Not as famous as his ancestor, nevertheless, he left a lasting legacy in zoology and in the conservation of the wild places of the world.

A version of this article appeared in the June 2017 e-newsletter of the Beverly Historical Society.

The Diplomat
By Terri McFadden

Beverly has had many noted residents over the years; one who contributed to the world stage during his long career was diplomat William Phillips. He was born in Beverly on May 30, 1878. The family summered in Beverly and lived the rest of the year in Boston at 299 Berkeley Street. But it was the family farm that William and his four siblings cherished as the highlight of their childhood. His father had established the farm off of Cabot Street next to Wenham Lake, not long after William's birth. Horseback riding, sailing and canoeing on the lake, fishing and swimming made for such ideal childhood activities that the children "never wanted to leave the place, even for an afternoon." They visited in the winter too, ice-boating and skating on the lake. The house was called "forest-lodge" in style, made of stone and wood with a brick terrace overlooking the lake.

Mr. Phillips attended Harvard College and following graduation attempted to get a position with John Hay, then Secretary of State – knocking on his door at 9:00 pm without invitation. Secretary Hay was gracious, but suggested to the young man he would be better off getting a law degree before trying to join the diplomatic corps. Although disappointed, Phillips took unenthusiastically the advice, attending Harvard Law. He studied there for 2 ½ "indifferent years." A visit to Biltmore in Ashville, North Carolina, changed his life. There he met Joseph Choate, Ambassador to Great Britain, who offered him a position on his staff.

Over the course of four decades diplomat William Phillips worked in the Department of State in China, Netherlands, Canada and Italy. He was twice the Assistant Secretary of State and was chief of the U.S. Office of Strategic Services during World War II. In 1946 he served on the Anglo-American Committee on Palestine, opposing the idea of partitioning the country.

He and his wife Caroline (Astor) Phillips had four children. When the couple retired the estate in Beverly became their year-round home. Phillips died in Sarasota, Florida in February 1968 and was buried in North Beverly Cemetery, not far from Moraine Farm where he had spent so many happy hours.

William and Caroline Phillips about 1960 on the terrace of their home at Moraine Farm. Right, the view of Wenham Lake from the terrace.

A version of this article appeared in the February 2016 e-newsletter of the Beverly Historical Society.

A Politician with a Heart
By Edward R. Brown

Daniel E. "Chick" McLean was a true son of Beverly's Goat Hill neighborhood, a corner of town that sticks out into the salt water river just before the Veterans Memorial Bridge. Until Bill Scanlon came on the scene in the 1990s, Chick was the dean of Beverly mayors, elected to an amazing six consecutive terms from 1936 until 1948.

"Chick," as everyone called him, acquired the nickname in his boyhood. Born in 1898, he grew up on Congress Street and spent all of his 82 years there. He was the son of Margaret and Daniel M. McLean – his dad was a Beverly police officer. Like many local young men of his time, he went to work at the United Shoe Machinery Corporation. He married Edith M. Holmes; they raised two daughters who would give them seven grandchildren. Since the United Shoe had built a golf course for its employees, Chick became an accomplished golfer and also enjoyed the occasional game of cards with friends at the 'Shoe" clubhouse. He also followed local sports avidly, and for many years seldom missed a Beverly High School football game.

He developed a passion for the local political scene. By the age of 30 he was elected to the Board of Aldermen (former name for the City Council), representing Ward 1. Until the ward lines were redrawn, Goat Hill was part of the same ward as Ryal Side.

Then in 1936, "Chick" ran for the mayor's office and was elected for the first time. He wouldn't leave the corner office on the third floor at City Hall until January of 1949. When Chick became mayor, America was still in the throes of the Great Depression. During the first term of his administration the federally financed Works Progress Administration did much work in the city, including the construction of Hurd Stadium as home for the football team. Soon on the heels of the Depression came World War II, when many hundreds of local residents went away to fight a war that had to be won, while loved ones left behind kept the home fires burning, the factories humming, and the Victory Gardens thriving. Through it all, Chick's steady leadership kept Beverly on a firm course and earned him the respect of just about everyone. He was re-elected every two years.

Chick McLean finally gave up the mayor's office at the end of 1948, deciding against a seventh term which he almost surely would have won. Still living on Congress Street, Chick accepted some new outside political challenges. Those included being town manager of Saugus, which changes town managers every year or so, and then city manager of Haverhill.

Beverly Mayor Daniel "Chick" McLean (far left) attending a Memorial Day Celebration in 1946.

He was appointed state chairman of the Massachusetts Appellate Tax Board. Governors would come and go, but whether a Democrat or a Republican occupied the State House, Chick stayed on the job for 19 years. Political to the core, he also found time to serve as chairman of the Republican State Committee from 1958 to 1960. Nevertheless, some of his best friends were Democrats. He kept up local organizational ties with the Elks Club, the Knights of Columbus, and the Beverly Golf and Tennis Club.

Jim Stommen, former editor of the Salem News, wrote this at the time of Chick's death in 1980: "Chick McLean was almost universally revered, to an extent that is unusual for one who devoted his life to the practice of politics......he was a man of the people, listening to their concerns and acting on them." This probably summed up the feelings of many people who remembered Chick, who long after he left office was still "Mr. Mayor" in Beverly.

A version of this article appeared in the November 2016 e-newsletter of the Beverly Historical Society.

www.ingramcontent.com/pod-product-compliance
Lightning Source LLC
Chambersburg PA
CBHW051803040426
42446CB00007B/494